GLENCOE

VOCABULARY BUILDER

Peter Fischer, Editorial Consultant

National-Louis University

Course 2

 **Glencoe**

New York, New York   Columbus, Ohio   Chicago, Illinois   Peoria, Illinois   Woodland Hills, California

Acknowledgments
The pronunciation key used in the glossary has been reproduced by permission
from *The American Heritage Dictionary of the English Language, Fourth Edition.*
Copyright © 2000 by Houghton Mifflin Company.

 **Glencoe**

The *McGraw-Hill* Companies

Printed in the United States of America

Send all inquiries to:
Glencoe/McGraw-Hill
8787 Orion Place
Columbus, OH 43240

SE ISBN: 0-07-861662-X
ATE ISBN: 0-07-861663-8

1 2 3 4 5 6 7 8 9 10 113 10 09 08 07 06 05 04

Contents

Name _____

Prometheus and Epimetheus

Zeus, the supreme ruler of the universe, with the aid of the giant Hercules and other gods, had rid the earth of the Titans and the Giants. The **expulsion** of these brutal creatures ensured that humans could now feel safe on Earth. The creation of humankind
5 was at hand.

Zeus, grateful for Prometheus's assistance in the war with the Titans, **delegated** the job of creating man to him and his brother Epimetheus. Prometheus was very wise and gave much **forethought** to this task. Epimetheus, on the other hand, was
10 not especially wise and tended to act without thinking.

So it was little wonder that Epimetheus thoughtlessly gave all the best gifts to the animals. He made them strong, fast, brave, and clever. He also **conferred** upon the animals fur, feathers, and shells. As a result, no great gifts remained to **bestow** on humans.
15 Without strength, bravery, cleverness, and a warm, protective coat, how could humans be protected from the animals?

Epimetheus sought out his brother Prometheus for help. Prometheus thought about the problem that Epimetheus had so recklessly caused and decided to grant man a splendid shape,
20 allowing him to stand erect like the gods. Then he brought fire down from the heavens and gave it to man. Fire was a far superior defense than anything given to the animals.

Zeus felt that Prometheus had been **excessively** generous to man in giving him fire. In addition, Zeus was angered that
25 Prometheus had arranged, by trickery, for man to get the best portion of sacrificed animals, while the gods got the worst parts. Zeus **retaliated** against this **maneuver** by creating Pandora, the first woman. She was beautiful, shy, and tempting to men and gods alike.
30 Zeus made a box for Pandora which held all the evils that could **befall** humans. In her curiosity, Pandora one day opened the box. Out came horrors that brought misery and calamity to humans. However, one good thing had been put in the box and was also released. That wondrous thing was Hope. Still today, hope remains humans' **consolation** amidst all the sufferings they must endure.

Words
befall
bestow
confer
consolation
delegate
excessive
expulsion
forethought
maneuver
retaliate

Each word in this lesson's word list appears in dark type in the selection you just read. Think about how the vocabulary word is used in the selection. Then write the letter for the best answer to each question.

1. Another word for *expulsion* in line 3 is _____.
   (A) glorification   (B) injury
   (C) removal   (D) discussion

   1. _____

2. If you *delegate* (line 7) a task, you _____.
   (A) praise it excessively (B) assign it to someone
   (C) lie about it   (D) discuss it with others

   2. _____

3. *Forethought* (line 9) means _____.
   (A) irrational fear   (B) excitement
   (C) exaggerated importance (D) preparation for the future

   3. _____

4. If you *confer* (line 13) something upon someone, you _____.
   (A) give an honor or gift (B) entrust someone with a secret
   (C) make a deal   (D) cause a disagreement

   4. _____

5. To *bestow* (line 14) is to _____.
   (A) attack   (B) request
   (C) punish   (D) grant

   5. _____

6. If something is *excessive* (line 23), it is _____.
   (A) openly brutal   (B) disgusting
   (C) more than reasonable   (D) embarrassing

   6. _____

7. If you *retaliate* (line 27), you _____.
   (A) wash thoroughly   (B) lean upon
   (C) push with great force (D) seek revenge

   7. _____

8. Which word could best replace *maneuver* in line 28?
   (A) response   (B) scheme
   (C) memory   (D) vehicle

   8. _____

9. *Befall* (line 31) means _____.
   (A) wish for   (B) stumble
   (C) happen to   (D) decrease

   9. _____

10. Another word for *consolation* in line 35 is _____.
    (A) comfort   (B) anger
    (C) confusion   (D) hunger

    10. _____

Applying Meaning

Decide which word in parentheses best completes the sentence. Then write the sentence, adding the missing word.

1. Since Mom can't clean the whole house herself, she _____ chores to each of us. (delegates; retaliates)

   _____

   _____

   _____

2. Pretending to be in a hurry was just a _____ to get to the front of the line. (forethought; maneuver)

   _____

   _____

   _____

3. The worrisome businessman always feared that financial misfortune would _____ his company. (bestow; befall)

   _____

   _____

   _____

4. The general _____ a great honor upon the soldier by presenting her with a medal. (retaliated; conferred)

   _____

   _____

   _____

5. The player's aggressive play eventually caused his _____ from the game. (consolation; expulsion)

   _____

   _____

   _____

6. I gave no _____ to my decision and ended up making the wrong choice. (forethought; delegation)

   _____

   _____

   _____

7. When the company cut its workers' vacation time, the employees
_____ by going on strike. (retaliated; conferred)

_____

_____

_____

8. Our only _____ after losing the game was that we had played well.
(expulsion; consolation)

_____

_____

_____

9. The generous king _____ great riches upon his most loyal subjects.
(bestowed; delegated)

_____

_____

_____

10. I thought his loud complaints to the store manager were _____ and
completely unnecessary. (excessive; conferred)

_____

_____

_____

Mastering Meaning

Greek mythology consists of a vast number of tales involving gods and goddesses who were divine beings endowed with superior attributes and immortality. Generally, each god or goddess had a special power or responsibility. For example, Poseidon, god of the sea, controlled and cared for the oceans. Other gods include Athena, the goddess of wisdom, and Ares, the god of war. Find and read myths about these and other gods; then make up a modern-day story in which one or more of these gods plays a central role. Use some of the words you studied in this lesson.

Vocabulary of Business

Name _____

In 1925, Calvin Coolidge said, "The business of the American people is business." Since colonial times, America has been a nation of industry and trade. Throughout the world, the United States is known as a country of economic prosperity and seemingly endless business opportunities. Accordingly, our language has numerous words appropriate for communicating ideas and concepts regarding the world of business. In this lesson, you will learn 10 words frequently used in the business world.

Unlocking Meaning

Read the sentences or short passages below. Write the letter for the correct definition of the italicized vocabulary word.

1. In earlier times, there was no currency. Instead, people would *barter*, offering goods or services in exchange for needed items.
   (A) to steal   (B) to borrow
   (C) to trade   (D) to pretend

2. In an effort to encourage repeat business, we mail coupons to all our previous *clients*.
   (A) relatives   (B) attorneys
   (C) criminals   (D) customers

3. To regulate extensive importing and exporting, the United States has numerous laws governing *commerce*.
   (A) the buying and selling of goods   (B) slow movement along a path
   (C) written orders or instructions   (D) the act of committing a crime

4. She worked diligently to complete the project. As *compensation* for her hard work, she was given an extra week of paid vacation.
   (A) a punishment or penalty   (B) literature published by a private individual
   (C) something given as payment or reward   (D) a public showing of sympathy

5. When we purchased a new computer system for our office, we hired a computer *consultant* to set up the system and train the staff to use it.
   (A) any person who buys a manufactured product   (B) one who gives professional or technical advice
   (C) an operator of machinery   (D) someone who assembles equipment

Words

- **barter**
- **client**
- **commerce**
- **compensation**
- **consultant**
- **inflation**
- **inventory**
- **investor**
- **overhead**
- **subsidize**

1. _____

2. _____

3. _____

4. _____

5. _____

6. To accommodate *inflation*, wages must rise accordingly.

(A) a slight decrease in yearly precipitation

(B) the addition of a synthetic substance to food

(C) exhaustion due to heavy labor

(D) an increase in prices

6. _____

7. When the shoe department's *inventory* runs low, the store's buyer purchases more shoes from suppliers.

(A) all the goods available for selling

(B) power or energy, such as electricity

(C) items still being developed

(D) salaries paid to employees

7. _____

8. When I wanted to start my own company, I needed money to purchase supplies and equipment. I asked my father if he wanted to be an *investor* in my business.

(A) one who purchases something in the hope of making a profit

(B) someone who researches an idea or proposal

(C) any person who gives authorization to pass business regulations

(D) a person who enters into an unsatisfactory agreement

8. _____

9. We paid the rent, electric, and telephone bills and our suppliers. The little we had left was our profit for the month. Those *overhead* expenses had taken almost half of the money in our account.

(A) responsibilities that have grown too large

(B) variables intended to alter the outcome of an experiment

(C) products that have outlived their usefulness

(D) general expenses of running a business

9. _____

10. Because the cost of producing milk made it too expensive for many families to buy, the government decided to *subsidize* dairy farmers in order to bring prices down.

(A) to impose legal fines

(B) to aid or assist with a grant of money

(C) to offer instruction or guidance

(D) to obstruct the supply of raw materials

10. _____

Applying Meaning

Follow the directions below to write a sentence using a vocabulary word.

1. Write a short job description for a position in a warehouse. Use the word *inventory* in your description.

   _____

   _____

   _____

2. Describe a typical day for a lawyer. Use a form of the word *client*.

   _____

   _____

   _____

3. Describe a conversation in which someone complains about the price of something. Use the word *inflation* in your sentence.

   _____

   _____

   _____

4. Describe an idea for a new invention. Use the word *investor*.

   _____

   _____

   _____

5. Write a sentence describing a doctor's office. Use the word *overhead*.

   _____

   _____

   _____

Decide which word in parentheses best completes the sentence. Then write the sentence, adding the missing word.

6. Martha hoped to _____ her fresh-baked bread for some fresh eggs and milk at the farm down the road. (subsidize; barter)

   _____

   _____

   _____

7. Because the factory manufactures equipment used by the postal service, it is _____ by the government. (bartered; subsidized)

_____

_____

_____

8. My mother, a financial _____, advises individuals on the best ways to invest their money. (client; consultant)

_____

_____

_____

9. The mill workers were offered a generous bonus as _____ for working on the holiday. (compensation; overhead)

_____

_____

_____

10. Interstate _____ nearly ground to a halt due to a strike in the shipping industry. (inflation; commerce)

_____

_____

_____

Cultural Literacy Note

The Midas Touch

In Greek mythology, King Midas ruled Phrygia, the land of roses. One day, Silenus, a follower of Dionysus, strayed into Midas's rose gardens. Midas returned him to Dionysus, the god of wine and revelry, who was so pleased to have Silenus back that he granted King Midas one wish. Midas wished that whatever he touched would turn to gold. Today, we refer to anyone who makes large amounts of money easily or establishes profitable businesses on a regular basis as having "the Midas touch."

Present a Report: Look through newspapers or magazines for an example of someone who, you think, has "the Midas touch." Report on him or her to the class.

Name _____

A *periscope* is a viewing instrument used when the direct line of vision is obstructed. It is a combination of the Greek *peri*, meaning "around," and the Greek *skopein*, meaning "to see." Literally, it is something used to "see around" things. Words containing the prefix *para-* come from the Greek word *para*, meaning "beside," "near," or "similar." This prefix is seen in words like *paralegal* and *paraphrase.* The vocabulary words in this lesson all have one of these prefixes.

Prefix	Meaning	Word
peri-	around	periscope
para-	near, beside similar	paraprofessional

Words

parable

paragraph

paralegal

paralysis

paramedic

paraphernalia

paraprofessional

parasite

perimeter

periodic

Unlocking Meaning

Write a vocabulary word that fits each clue below. Then say the word and write a short definition. Compare your definition with the one in the back of the book.

1. It contains the Greek root *graphein*, meaning "to write." It literally means "to write beside."

   _____

   _____

   _____

2. This word might be used to identify someone who works "beside" a lawyer, a doctor, or another professional.

   _____

   _____

   _____

3. This person's work is "similar" to that of a medical doctor.

   _____

   _____

   _____

4. This word comes from the Greek word *paraluein*, meaning "to loosen or disable." It can be the result of injury or fear.

_____

_____

_____

5. It combines the prefix *peri-* with the Greek word *metron*, meaning "measure." It is something you might study in geometry.

_____

_____

_____

6. This word originated with the Greek *paraballein*, meaning "to compare." The Bible contains many of these.

_____

_____

_____

7. This might be used to describe someone who works "near" an attorney-at-law.

_____

_____

_____

8. It comes from *peri-* and the Greek *hodos*, meaning "way." Its current meaning suggests coming around again and again.

_____

_____

_____

9. The Greek word *pherne* appearing in this word originally referred to a woman's dowry. Now it has a more general meaning.

_____

_____

_____

10. This word includes the Greek *sitos*, meaning "grain" or "food." Someone who sits at someone else's table and eats that person's food might be called this.

_____

_____

_____

Applying Meaning

Follow the directions below to write a sentence using a vocabulary word.

1. Write a short description of a biology study. Use the word *parasite* in your description.

   _____

   _____

   _____

2. Write a sentence about a person's career. Use the word *paraprofessional*.

   _____

   _____

   _____

3. Describe a conversation in which someone tells a story. Use the word *parable* in your sentence.

   _____

   _____

   _____

4. Describe a backyard garden. Use the word *perimeter*.

   _____

   _____

   _____

5. Write a sentence describing a scene in an emergency room. Use the word *paramedic* in your description.

   _____

   _____

   _____

6. Describe a photographer's attic or basement. Use the word *paraphernalia*.

   _____

   _____

   _____

7. Write a sentence about a performer who experiences extreme stage fright. Use the word *paralysis*.

_____

_____

_____

Write a vocabulary word to complete each statement.

8. *Letter* is to *word* as *sentence* is to _____.

9. *Always* is to *sometimes* as *constant* is to _____.

10. *Professor* is to *teaching assistant* as *lawyer* is to _____.

8. _____

9. _____

10. _____

Bonus Word

paradise

Paradise comes from an ancient Persian word meaning "enclosed place." Made up of a prefix meaning "around" and a root meaning "wall," *pairi-daeza* literally meant "a place with a wall around it." Eventually, this term came to apply to enclosed gardens and parks. In the Greek version of the Bible, this word was applied to the Garden of Eden. As Eden has come to be synonymous with blissful places, it is only natural that the early word for this perfect garden describes any place of perfect happiness and pleasure.

Use Your Dictionary: Find additional words beginning with the *para-* and *peri-* prefixes. For each word you find, write a sentence that demonstrates the meaning of the word.

Name _____

How well do you remember the words you studied in Lessons 1 through 3? Take the following test covering the words from the last three lessons.

Part 1 Choose the Correct Meaning

Each question below includes a word in capital letters, followed by four words or phrases. Choose the word or phrase that is <u>closest</u> in meaning to the word in capital letters. Write the letter for your answer on the line provided.

Sample

| S. FINISH | (A) enjoy | (B) complete | S. _____ |
| | (C) destroy | (D) enlarge | |

| 1. PERIMETER | (A) area | (B) length | 1. _____ |
| | (C) boundary | (D) volume | |

| 2. FORETHOUGHT | (A) absentmindedness | (B) planning | 2. _____ |
| | (C) agreement | (D) understanding | |

| 3. INFLATION | (A) price change | (B) price increase | 3. _____ |
| | (C) price decrease | (D) savings | |

| 4. PARABLE | (A) chart | (B) graph | 4. _____ |
| | (C) story | (D) picture | |

| 5. CONFER | (A) give | (B) praise | 5. _____ |
| | (C) seek | (D) congratulate | |

| 6. PARAMEDIC | (A) nurse | (B) pharmacist | 6. _____ |
| | (C) orderly | (D) medical assistant | |

| 7. RETALIATE | (A) review | (B) return | 7. _____ |
| | (C) thank | (D) get revenge | |

| 8. CONSULTANT | (A) professional | (B) employee | 8. _____ |
| | (C) advisor | (D) trainee | |

| 9. BEFALL | (A) occur | (B) push | 9. _____ |
| | (C) restrain | (D) avoid | |

| 10. COMMERCE | (A) advertising | (B) trade | 10. _____ |
| | (C) movement | (D) tourism | |

11. PERIODIC (A) final   (B) repeated   11. _____
       (C) temporary (D) unusual

12. OVERHEAD (A) rent   (B) budget   12. _____
       (C) charges   (D) operating costs

13. PARALEGAL (A) lawyer's assistant (B) outside the law 13. _____
       (C) against the law (D) police

14. CONSOLATION (A) comfort   (B) response   14. _____
       (C) thought   (D) hope

15. MANEUVER (A) hike   (B) feeling   15. _____
       (C) move   (D) cover-up

Part 2 Matching Words and Meanings

Match the definition in Column B with the word in Column A. Write
the letter of the correct definition on the line provided.

Column A	Column B	
16. delegate	a. give or present	16. _____
17. paraphernalia	b. too much	17. _____
18. excessive	c. customer	18. _____
19. subsidize	d. payment	19. _____
20. parasite	e. loss of motion	20. _____
21. barter	f. assign	21. _____
22. paralysis	g. trade	22. _____
23. compensation	h. support with money	23. _____
24. bestow	i. something that lives off something else	24. _____
25. client	j. personal belongings, equipment	25. _____

Name _____

The Teapot Dome Affair

As long as there have been governments, there have been scandals and corruption. Politicians and their **associates** have taken part in bribery, extortion, criminal conspiracy, and other immoral and illegal activities. Warren G. Harding's presidency is considered by
5 some to be one of the most corrupt **administrations** in American history.

The most notorious of the Harding scandals is known as the Teapot Dome Affair. Teapot Dome, Wyoming, was named for a rock that sat on the land and resembled a teapot. This parcel of
10 land contained oil that had been **allocated** to the United States Navy for its future needs. The oil was to be kept in its natural **reservoir** until it was required for use by United States naval vessels.

Numerous conservation policies, including the petroleum reserve
15 policy, assigned control of tracts of land to the federal government. Opposition to the petroleum reserve policy was strong among private oil interests. For the sake of profit, they argued that the navy's needs could be better met through the private **enterprise** of American oil companies.

20 Harding's secretary of the interior, Albert B. Fall, a longtime **disputant** in the petroleum reserve policy debate, persuaded the secretary of the navy to turn over the management of these federally owned oil reserve sites to the Department of the Interior. Fall then secretly leased the sites to private companies in return for
25 bribes. He leased Teapot Dome to the Mammoth Oil Company and another oil reserve to the Pan-American Petroleum Company.

The full story became public after Harding's death in 1923. Later that year, the Senate conducted an investigation. Close **scrutiny** revealed that when the leases were signed, Fall had received an
30 extremely large, interest-free loan from the president of the Pan-American Petroleum Company. He also received a large amount of cash and government bonds directly from the president of Mammoth Oil. These payments totaled more than $400,000.

As a **consequence** of these findings, Congress agreed to sue
35 for cancellation of the leases. In addition to **rescinding** the leases, the government charged Fall and others involved in the incident with conspiracy to defraud the government. They were eventually **acquitted**, but Fall was also charged with bribery and found guilty. He served one year in prison and was fined $100,000.

Words
acquit
administration
allocate
associate
consequence
disputant
enterprise
rescind
reservoir
scrutiny

Each word in this lesson's word list appears in dark type in the selection you just read. Think about how the vocabulary word is used in the selection. Then write the letter for the best answer to each question.

1. An *associate* (line 2) is a(n) _____.
   (A) staff
   (B) rival
   (C) impersonator
   (D) coworker

   1. _____

2. An *administration* (line 5) is a(n) _____.
   (A) group of officials in charge of managing a government
   (B) library of reference materials and educational texts
   (C) organized system of highways and secondary roads
   (D) collection of publicly owned properties

   2. _____

3. Which word could best replace *allocated* in line 10?
   (A) built
   (B) assigned
   (C) borrowed
   (D) destroyed

   3. _____

4. A *reservoir* (line 12) is a(n) _____.
   (A) place where a liquid is stored
   (B) landing strip for aircraft
   (C) official uniform
   (D) laboratory

   4. _____

5. An *enterprise* (line 18) is a(n) _____.
   (A) reward for good service
   (B) secret passage
   (C) activity designed to make money
   (D) expensive luxury

   5. _____

6. If you are a *disputant* (line 21), you are _____.
   (A) a registered voter
   (B) guilty of a crime
   (C) a government official
   (D) involved in an argument

   6. _____

7. Which word could best replace *scrutiny* in line 28?
   (A) examination
   (B) friendship
   (C) digestion
   (D) battle

   7. _____

8. Which word could best replace *consequence* in line 34?
   (A) beginning
   (B) denial
   (C) repeat
   (D) result

   8. _____

9. Another word for *rescinding* in line 35 is _____.
   (A) applauding
   (B) revoking
   (C) balancing
   (D) reviewing

   9. _____

10. *Acquitted* (line 38) means _____.
    (A) misplaced
    (B) taken on a journey
    (C) found not guilty
    (D) asked to respond

    10. _____

Name _____

Applying Meaning

Follow the directions below to write a sentence using a vocabulary word.

1. Use any form of the word *acquit* in a sentence about a jury trial.

_____
_____
_____

2. Use any form of the word *associate* in a sentence about a group of workers.

_____
_____
_____

3. Use any form of the word *disputant* to describe an argument you witnessed.

_____
_____
_____

4. Use any form of the word *rescind* to describe what happened after an automobile accident.

_____
_____
_____

5. Use *consequence* in a sentence about a change in the weather.

_____
_____
_____

Read each sentence below. Write "correct" on the answer line if the vocabulary word has been used correctly or "incorrect" if it has been used incorrectly.

6. When the angry protesters arrived at the meeting, they were *allocated* from the hall by security guards.

6. _____

7. The President began appointing the members to his new *administration* soon after he was inaugurated.

7. _____

8. It takes an *enterprising* person to work hard and start a successful business.

8. _____

9. Since the *reservoir* supplies the town's drinking water, it is tested weekly for contamination.

9. _____

10. The sailors, fed up with their captain's tyranny, initiated a *scrutiny* against him.

10. _____

For each word used incorrectly, write a sentence using the word properly.

_____

_____

_____

_____

_____

_____

_____

_____

_____

Mastering Meaning

An infamous example of corruption in American history is the Tweed Ring, a group led by a man named William Marcy Tweed in the late 1800s. "Boss" Tweed, the Democratic boss of New York City, and his associates put together a plan involving the use of the city's funds. Tweed arranged for companies he owned to receive most of the city's contracts. In this way, and by other fraudulent means, Tweed accumulated large sums of money. Eventually, he was arrested and sued by the state of New York. Write a brief editorial for a newspaper, discussing your opinion of a real or fictitious instance of political corruption. Use some of the words you studied in this lesson.

Vocabulary of Appearance

Name _____

You have probably heard the saying, "A picture is worth a thousand words." Sometimes, however, one word can go a long way toward describing the appearance of a person, a place, or a thing. For example, a single word like *ornate* or *gaudy* can tell you a great deal about something. It can also reveal the user's attitude toward what he or she sees. In this lesson, you will learn 10 words that describe appearance.

Unlocking Meaning

Words
commonplace
elaborate
gaudy
lustrous
mediocre
ornate
shoddy
sleazy
slipshod
squalid

Read the sentences or short passages below. Write the letter for the correct definition of the italicized word.

1. My story was rejected by the publisher, who said my plot and characters were so *commonplace* that no one would bother to read very far.
   (A) unusual   (B) ordinary
   (C) exciting   (D) mysterious

2. After spending months making *elaborate* plans for the festival, it seemed foolish to cancel it because of a little rain.
   (A) brief   (B) expensive
   (C) highly detailed   (D) unusable

1. _____

3. After moving into the apartment, we covered up the *gaudy* red, green, and silver-colored walls with a coat of plain gray paint.
   (A) tastelessly colorful   (B) simple
   (C) youthful   (D) awe-inspiring

2. _____

4. Eduardo was startled by the *lustrous* green eyes of our cat when he pointed his flashlight into the dark room.
   (A) darkened   (B) watery
   (C) shining   (D) exciting

3. _____

5. After getting all C's on his report card, Dan vowed he would improve on his *mediocre* performance.
   (A) exception   (B) remarkable
   (C) pleasant   (D) neither good nor bad

4. _____

5. _____

6. While their subjects lived in plain, often impoverished circumstances, the royal family was surrounded by *ornate* rooms decorated with expensive paintings and custom-made furniture.
   (A) small   (B) highly decorated
   (C) plain   (D) foreign

6. _____

7. Henry always paid more to get the best possible appliances. He felt paying less for *shoddy* merchandise that constantly needed repairs was no bargain.

    (A) pretty   (B) unusual

    (C) imported   (D) poor quality

    7. _____

8. The candidate accused the present mayor of running a *sleazy* administration, full of payoffs and backroom deals with organized crime.

    (A) corrupt   (B) honest

    (C) democratic   (D) powerful

    8. _____

9. In the dangerous job of generating nuclear energy, there is no room for a *slipshod* performance by any worker in the plant.

    (A) slippery   (B) professional

    (C) careless   (D) outstanding

    9. _____

10. Mother Teresa devoted her life to aiding the poor in the *squalid* slums of Calcutta.

    (A) wretched and repulsive   (B) hidden

    (C) widespread   (D) devout

    10. _____

Applying Meaning

Each question below contains a vocabulary word from this lesson.
Answer each question "yes" or "no" in the space provided.

1. Could a bright purple and orange hat with large pink ostrich feathers
   be described as *gaudy*?

   1. _____

2. Would it be reasonable to say that a perfect score on a test is
   mediocre?

   2. _____

3. Is it *commonplace* for one person to win three gold medals at the
   Olympics?

   3. _____

4. Is a highly polished diamond usually *lustrous*?

   4. _____

5. Would you expect a fine restaurant to prepare food in a *squalid*
   kitchen?

   5. _____

For each question you answered "no," write a sentence explaining
your reason.

_____
_____
_____
_____
_____
_____
_____
_____

Write a sentence following the directions below.

6. Use the word *elaborate* to describe a plan.

_____
_____
_____

7. Write a sentence describing a piece of artwork. Use the word *ornate*.

_____
_____
_____

8. Write a sentence about an absent-minded professor. Use the word *slipshod* in your sentence.

_____

_____

_____

9. Use the word *sleazy* to describe a character in a movie, book, or play.

_____

_____

_____

10. Use the word *shoddy* to describe an article of clothing.

_____

_____

_____

The Dictionary

The dictionary uses a special alphabet called a phonetic alphabet to help you pronounce words correctly. Each symbol in a phonetic alphabet stands for one and only one sound. For example, the letter *c* in our alphabet may be represented by an *s*, for the sound you hear at the beginning of *cent*, or by a *k*, for the sound that begins the word *cat*.

Word	Phonetic Spelling
cent	(sent)
cat	(kat)

Check the Phonetic Spelling: Write the normal spelling for these phonetic spellings. Refer to the phonetic chart in the dictionary at the back of the book.

āt	{ate or eight}	prǐ **pâr'**	{prepare}
rān	{rain}	gärd	{guard}
sīn	{sign}	**kăm'** ər ə	{camera}
kou	{cow}	ə **ka'** zhən	{occasion}

The Roots -graph-, -scribe-, and -script-

Name _____

The old-fashioned, elaborate writing you often see on invitations and certificates is called *calligraphy*. The word *calligraphy* comes from the Greek word *kallos*, meaning "beautiful," and the Greek verb *graphein*, which means "to write." Many other English words associated with writing or drawing contain the Greek root *-graph-*. Words containing the Latin roots *-scribe-* or *-script-* come from the Latin verb *scribere*, meaning "to write." These roots are seen in words like *describe* and *manuscript*. Each vocabulary word in this lesson has one of these Greek or Latin roots.

Root	Meaning	Word
graphien	to write	graphic
scribere	to write	subscribe

Unlocking Meaning

Write a vocabulary word for each of these definitions or clues. Then rewrite the definition in your own words. Use the dictionary in the back of the book to check your answer.

1. This word begins with the Latin prefix *in-*, meaning "in."

   _____

   _____

   _____

2. You might recognize the Greek word *topos*, meaning "place" in this word.

   _____

   _____

   _____

3. The prefix in this word is also found in words like *submit* and *submarine*. When you promise to pay for a magazine or a charitable contribution, you might be asked to sign your name at the bottom of your promise.

   _____

   _____

   _____

Words

cinematographer

graphic

inscribe

oceanography

prescribe

seismograph

subscribe

topography

transcript

typography

4. Part of this word comes from *Oceanus*, the Greek god of the sea.

_____

_____

_____

5. It literally means "to write out beforehand." It usually refers to a rule or command.

_____

_____

_____

6. This word includes the Greek word *kinema*, meaning "motion," as in motion picture.

_____

_____

_____

7. Part of this word comes from the Greek word *seiein*, meaning "to shake." It is usually applied to the shaking of the ground.

_____

_____

_____

8. The Greek word *typos*, meaning "impression," is found in this word used to describe a type of printing.

_____

_____

_____

9. If your handwriting is bad, you might need one of these to "transport" its meaning to yourself and others.

_____

_____

_____

10. As a noun, it might refer to a picture. As an adjective, it might be used to describe something very clearly shown.

_____

_____

_____

Applying Meaning

Decide which word in parentheses best completes the sentence. Then write the sentence, adding the missing word.

1. Before our hiking trip, we wanted to learn the _____ of the region, so we consulted a map to locate canyons and cliffs. (typography; topography)

   _____

   _____

   _____

2. We bought a silver bracelet for Mother and took it to an engraver to have it _____ with her name. (inscribed; prescribed)

   _____

   _____

   _____

3. My parents _____ to several professional journals as well as to magazines such as *Time* and *National Geographic*. (subscribe; inscribe)

   _____

   _____

   _____

4. Jacques Cousteau, the world-famous _____, was a pioneer in undersea exploration and spent his career studying sea life. (typographer; oceanographer)

   _____

   _____

   _____

5. After the student council meeting, the secretary used his notes to type up an official _____ of everything that was said. (transcript; seismograph)

   _____

   _____

   _____

Write a vocabulary word to complete each statement.

6. *Poet* is to *poetic* as graph is to _____.

6. _____

7. *Book* is to *author* as *movie* is to _____.

7. _____

8. *Temperature* is to *thermometer* as *earthquake* is to _____.

8. _____

9. *Camera* is to *photography* as *printing press* is to _____.

9. _____

10. *Description* is to *describe* as *prescription* is to _____.

10. _____

Test-Taking Strategies

In analogy tests you are asked to choose a pair of words with the same relationship to each other as another pair of words. To complete these analogies, think carefully about how the given pair of words relate to each other and then choose the pair that best expresses the same relationship.

Example:

TREE : LEAF   (A) JAR : LID   (B) HAMMER : NAIL

E. _____

(C) BOOK : PAGE   (D) GRASS : YARD

Don't be tricked by the order of the words. For example, grass and yard go from a small element, the grass, to a larger element, the yard. The relationship of a tree and a leaf, however, is from the tree to its smaller element, the leaf.

Practice: For each item below, select the pair of words that best matches the relationship of the original pair of words.

1. PILOT : PLANE   (A) lawyer : judge   (B) captain : ship

1. _____

(C) farmer : crops   (D) actor : script

2. SENTENCE : PARAGRAPH   (A) title : author   (B) page : topic

(C) letter : word   (D) book : chapter

2. _____

3. BRUSH : PAINT   (A) water : bucket   (B) pencil : drawing

(C) yard : rake   (D) knife : butter

3. _____

Name _____

How well do you remember the words you studied in Lessons 4 through 6? Take the following test covering the words from the last three lessons.

Part 1 Antonyms

Each question below includes a word in capital letters, followed by four words or phrases. Choose the word or phrase that is most nearly <u>opposite</u> in meaning to the word in capital letters. Write the letter for your answer on the line provided.

Sample

S. SLOW	(A) lazy	(B) simple	S. _____
	(C) fast	(D) common	

1. SQUALID	(A) tidy	(B) flat	1. _____
	(C) cold	(D) old	

2. RESCIND	(A) uphold	(B) alter	2. _____
	(C) copy	(D) vote on	

3. COMMONPLACE	(A) privately owned	(B) boring	3. _____
	(C) mysterious	(D) unusual	

4. TRANSCRIPT	(A) book	(B) original	4. _____
	(C) copy	(D) translation	

5. LUSTROUS	(A) colorful	(B) dull	5. _____
	(C) metallic	(D) multicolored	

6. CONSEQUENCE	(A) result	(B) punishment	6. _____
	(C) plan	(D) cause	

7. SLEAZY	(A) dirty	(B) illegal	7. _____
	(C) hidden	(D) honest	

8. ACQUIT	(A) detain	(B) question	8. _____
	(C) convict	(D) release	

9. ELABORATE	(A) simple	(B) inexpensive	9. _____
	(C) comprehensive	(D) detailed	

10. SCRUTINY	(A) testing	(B) cleaning	10. _____
	(C) instructing	(D) overlooking	

11. MEDIOCRE   (A) complex   (B) exceptional   11. _____

                       (C) new   (D) fresh

12. GAUDY   (A) colorful   (B) childlike   12. _____

                       (C) plain   (D) empty

13. SHODDY   (A) well-liked   (B) forgotten   13. _____

                       (C) thick   (D) high-quality

14. SLIPSHOD   (A) harmless   (B) careful   14. _____

                       (C) old-fashioned   (D) temporary

15. ORNATE   (A) simple   (B) handmade   15. _____

                       (C) machine-made   (D) useful

Part 2 Matching Words and Meanings

Match the definition in Column B with the word in Column A. Write the letter of the correct definition on the line provided.

Column A	**Column B**	
16. oceanography	a. mapped features of the earth	16. _____
17. associate	b. instrument that measures movement	17. _____
18. seismograph	c. direct	18. _____
19. disputant	d. study of the ocean	19. _____
20. administration	e. person who makes movies	20. _____
21. cinematographer	f. project	21. _____
22. enterprise	g. person engaged in an argument	22. _____
23. prescribe	h. coworker	23. _____
24. allocate	i. assign	24. _____
25. topography	j. people who manage or govern	25. _____

Name _____

Hole in the Sky

Millions of years ago, the earth experienced a catastrophe that resulted in massive global cooling. Eventually, all the earth's water froze. This **era** is known as the Ice Age. Scientists believe that a meteor struck the earth with such force that it sent a great cloud of
5 dust into the earth's atmosphere, effectively blocking the sun's light and heat. This in turn caused the earth's temperature to drop low enough to cause global freezing. After many years, the dust cleared from the atmosphere. Once again the sun's warmth was able to **penetrate** the clouds. The ice melted, except at the earth's two
10 poles—areas too far from the sun to experience temperatures high enough to cause **thawing**.

    The climate of the earth is **precisely** balanced to support a variety of life forms that depend on a range of temperatures. These temperatures range from extremely cold at the poles to extremely
15 hot near the center of the earth at the **equator**. The layers of the earth's atmosphere act as a filter to allow only as much sunlight as needed to maintain this balance. Unfortunately, the growth of fuel-burning industries and an increase in previously unknown **synthetic** compounds have altered this filter.

20   The layer of the atmosphere that screens excessive sunlight is the ozone layer. Ozone is a compound made up of three oxygen molecules. It tends to break down when it is attacked by chlorine, a chemical released by the propellants in aerosol sprays and coolants in air-conditioning units. Widespread use of aerosol sprays
25 and air conditioning has already caused **irreversible** damage to the ozone layer.

    Over the South Pole, scientists have found a reduction in the amount of atmospheric ozone. This hole in the earth's natural filter allows more sunlight to **infiltrate** the atmosphere. This in turn af-
30 fects the global climate. The resulting warming is suspected to be the cause of numerous incidents, from the melting of the polar ice caps to an increase in tropical storms. These and other **meteoro-logical** events all threaten to disturb the balance the earth's climate must maintain. If this balance is disrupted, life forms all over the
35 planet will be affected.

    Numerous scientific and environmental groups have asked that people **forswear** the use of aerosol sprays and certain coolants in the hopes of halting the dangerous loss of ozone in our atmosphere.

Words

equator

era

forswear

infiltrate

irreversible

meteorological

penetrate

precise

synthetic

thaw

Each word in this lesson's word list appears in dark type in the selection you just read. Think about how the vocabulary word is used in the selection. Then write the letter for the best answer to each question.

1. Another word for *era* in line 3 is _____.   1. _____
   (A) air   (B) calendar
   (C) time   (D) happiness

2. If something *penetrates* a thing (line 9), it _____.   2. _____
   (A) crystallizes   (B) goes through it
   (C) seeks shelter   (D) absorbs it

3. *Thawing* (line 11) means _____.   3. _____
   (A) growing   (B) searching
   (C) melting   (D) moving

4. Which word could best replace *precisely* in line 12?   4. _____
   (A) slowly   (B) secretly
   (C) periodically   (D) exactly

5. The *equator* (line 15) is _____.   5. _____
   (A) the imaginary line around   (B) the brightest star in the
       the center of the earth   northern hemisphere
   (C) the most active volcano on   (D) a canyon at the bottom
       the earth   of the ocean

6. Which word could best replace *synthetic* in line 19?   6. _____
   (A) complicated   (B) explosive
   (C) pitiful   (D) artificial

7. Something that is *irreversible* (line 25) is _____.   7. _____
   (A) barely within reach   (B) permanent and unchangeable
   (C) suspected to be a mistake (D) able to adapt quickly

8. *Infiltrate* (line 29) means _____.   8. _____
   (A) wipe out   (B) filter through
   (C) enlarge   (D) attack

9. *Meteorological* (line 32) means _____.   9. _____
   (A) having to do with space   (B) having to do with measurements
   (C) having to do with cattle (D) having to do with weather

10. Another word for *forswear* (line 37) is _____.   10. _____
    (A) reject   (B) embrace
    (C) encourage   (D) divide

Applying Meaning

Decide which word in parentheses best completes the sentence. Then write the sentence, adding the missing word.

1. The _____ fibers in this jacket have been designed to resist moisture and hold heat better than any natural fibers. (irreversible; synthetic)

_____

_____

_____

2. I made a chart to track _____ trends such as rainfall, temperature, and humidity for one month. (meteorological; synthetic)

_____

_____

_____

3. After he gained twelve pounds, Judd decided to _____ all junk food and sweets. (forswear; infiltrate)

_____

_____

_____

4. In spite of our pleas, the principal's decision remained _____. (irreversible; precise)

_____

_____

_____

5. She mixed the _____ amount of sugar, flour, and salt called for in the recipe. (precise; synthetic)

_____

_____

_____

Read each sentence below. Write "correct" on the answer line if the vocabulary word has been used correctly or "incorrect" if it has been used incorrectly.

6. As the ship sailed across the *equator*, the captain announced that we had entered the Southern Hemisphere.

6. _____

7. The typist made an *era* in spelling when she typed the document.

7. _____

8. Before dropping the time capsule into the lake, we welded the container shut so no water could *penetrate* it and destroy the contents.

8. _____

9. Gradually the rain began to *infiltrate* the parched ground and nourish the nearly dead crops.

9. _____

10. The water was placed in the freezer to *thaw* in time for the party.

10. _____

For each word used incorrectly, write a sentence using the word properly.

_____ _____

_____

_____

_____

_____

_____

_____

_____

_____

_____

_____

Mastering Meaning

As a result of ignorance, negligence, and, in some cases, outright abuse, the delicate balance of nature on our planet has been threatened. Natural resources have been depleted; species of plants and animals face extinction; and our air and water suffer from the effects of pollutants. Fortunately, increased awareness has caused new laws and programs to be enacted to protect the environment. Think about environmental issues you have heard or read about. Choose the one that concerns you most. Write a short paper explaining why people should embrace and support this issue. Use some of the words you studied in this lesson.

Vocabulary of Anger and Violence

Name _____

We live in a violent world. News reports and television documentaries present images of war, natural disasters, and every imaginable type of conflict. Journalists can draw on many words in the English language to describe the anger and violence that characterize these situations. In this lesson, you will learn 10 words relating to anger and violence.

Unlocking Meaning

A vocabulary word appears in italics in each short passage below. Think about how the word is used in the passage and write a short definition of it. Compare your definition with the one given in the dictionary at the back of the book.

Words
brutish
harass
lacerate
lambaste
maim
mutilate
rile
skirmish
tantrum
taunt

1. The gangster threatened the prosecutor's family, but she was used to such *brutish* behavior and refused to drop the charges.

   _____

   _____

   _____

2. A few hecklers attempted to *harass* the speaker by shouting slogans and blowing whistles during his speech.

   _____

   _____

   _____

3. As the television newscaster reported on the hurricane, a gust of wind blew out a nearby window, and flying glass *lacerated* her arm.

   _____

   _____

   _____

4. The governor grew tired of the newspaper's negative editorials, so in his press conference he began to *lambaste* both the owners and editors.

   _____

   _____

   _____

5. The motorcyclist's leg was badly *maimed* when he slid off the road. Doctors may need to amputate if it does not respond to treatment.

_____

_____

_____

6. A person who fills out a form is often directed not to bend or *mutilate* it.

_____

_____

_____

7. We watched the puppy try to *rile* the older dogs by hopping on their backs and biting their tails.

_____

_____

_____

8. The conflict on this battlefield was only a *skirmish*. The real battle happened 10 miles away.

_____

_____

_____

9. After his humiliating defeat, the coach lost control and threw a *tantrum*, stamping his feet and screaming hysterically at the players.

_____

_____

_____

10. When the guide saw the boy throwing pebbles through the fence, she warned him not to *taunt* the bear.

_____

_____

_____

Applying Meaning

Read each sentence below. Write "correct" on the answer line if the vocabulary word has been used correctly or "incorrect" if it has been used incorrectly.

1. I'm really a little *skirmish* about snakes. I don't mind looking at them if they're behind glass, but I would never want to hold one.

2. The store's owner said we could hand out pamphlets in front of his shop as long as we didn't *harass* any of his customers.

3. The recipe said to put the roast in the oven and *lambaste* it every hour.

4. The fans like to *taunt* the members of the opposing team by chanting "Who cares?" as each player is introduced.

5. Before entering an unfamiliar area, it is wise to *maim* the bushes to scare off any animals lurking there.

1. _____

2. _____

3. _____

4. _____

5. _____

For each word used incorrectly, write a sentence using the word correctly.

_____
_____
_____
_____
_____
_____
_____
_____
_____
_____
_____
_____

Write a sentence following the directions below.

6. Use the word *brutish* in a sentence about the actions of someone you read or know about.

_____
_____
_____

7. Write a sentence warning someone about a broken window. Use any form of the word *lacerate*.

_____

_____

_____

8. Use any form of the word *mutilate* to describe an encounter between two animals in the wild.

_____

_____

_____

9. Write a sentence about something that happened to you. Use any form of the word *rile*.

_____

_____

_____

10. Describe a small child's behavior. Use the word *tantrum*.

_____

_____

_____

Our Living Language

When reporting the results of sporting events, sportscasters often describe the outcomes with words we typically associate with anger or violence. How many times have you heard a sports reporter say that one team "smashed" another team's defenses or that a team suffered a "crushing" blow?

Cooperative Learning: Work with a partner to write a script to report the results of the weekend's games. Use some of the words you studied in this lesson. Then read your sports report to the class.

Number Prefixes and Roots

Name _____

Many words in the English language begin with a prefix or root that is derived from a Latin or Greek word for a number. Knowing these prefixes and roots can help you understand the meaning of a word. Study the examples below.

Prefix or Root	Meaning	Word
mono-	single, alone	monarchy
uni-	one	uniformity
deca-	ten	decathlon
centum	hundred	centenary
hex-	six	hexagon
novem	nine	novena
octo-	eight	octagonal
sex-	six	sextuplet

Words

centenary

decathlon

hexagon

monarchy

monotonous

novena

octagonal

quadruple

sextet

uniformity

Unlocking Meaning

A vocabulary word appears in italics in each sentence or short passage below. Find the root in each vocabulary word and choose the letter for the correct definition. Write the letter for your answer on the line provided.

1. The *century* following the Civil War brought numerous changes in American life. By 1965 jet travel and mass production had become common.
   (A) cost of goods   (B) 100 years
   (C) 10 years   (D) five cents

   1. _____

2. Requiring a variety of skills, the *decathlon* is one of the great challenges of the competition.
   (A) a five part-announcement   (B) a contest lasting two hours
   (C) a 100-mile race   (D) a contest made up of 10 events

   2. _____

3. The cake was baked in the shape of a *hexagon* and decorated to look like a birthday card.
   (A) a figure with six sides   (B) a square
   (C) a star   (D) a circle

   3. _____

4. All the lords and lower nobility swore their loyalty to the power and authority of the *monarchy*.
   (A) rule by a committee of four people   (B) a type of bridge
   (C) government by one person   (D) police state

   4. _____

5. After a week the diet of green vegetables became quite *monotonous*.
   (A) characterized by variety   (B) two-sided
   (C) dull due to the repetition   (D) mountainous
       of one thing

5. _____

6. The *novena* to St. Jude will begin on Tuesday and end a week from
   Wednesday.
   (A) nine days of prayer   (B) weekly report
   (C) new song   (D) annual event

6. _____

7. The problem required that we calculate the surface area of an
   octagonal conference table.
   (A) shaped like an octopus   (B) eight-sided
   (C) made up of 10 parts   (D) lopsided

7. _____

8. The financial advisor claimed he was able to *quadruple* his money
   in two years.
   (A) multiply by four   (B) double
   (C) cut in half   (D) lose

8. _____

9. Some members of the band decided to form a *sextet* to provide
   entertainment at weddings and similar events.
   (A) a group of religious officials   (B) a troupe of 16 dancers
   (C) people engaged in illegal   (D) a group of six
       activity

9. _____

10. The *uniformity* in the size and shape of each plank in the board-
    walk was the result of the carpenter's careful measurements.
    (A) dull covering   (B) simplicity
    (C) sameness   (D) variety

10. _____

Applying Meaning

Follow the directions below to write a sentence using a vocabulary word.

1. Use the word *monotonous* in a sentence about the weather.

   _____

   _____

   _____

2. Write a description about a government, using the word *monarchy*.

   _____

   _____

   _____

3. Write a sentence about a track-and field competition. Use the word *decathlon*.

   _____

   _____

   _____

4. Write a sentence describing one or more buildings, using any form of the word *uniformity*.

   _____

   _____

   _____

5. Use the word *centenary* in a sentence about a celebration.

   _____

   _____

   _____

Read each sentence or short passage below. Write "correct" on the answer line if the vocabulary word has been used correctly or "incorrect" if it has been used incorrectly.

6. Using a powerful telescope, the astronomers found a previously undiscovered *novena* in a distant region of the galaxy.

   6. _____

7. Juan used a computer to add two sides to the square to form a *hexagon*.

   7. _____

8. The ten sides of the *octagonal* figure measured a total of 29 inches.

8. _____

9. The navigator felt he should check the ship's position with his *sextet* instead of relying entirely on his computer.

9. _____

10. Last year, we got only 12 tomatoes from our garden. This spring, we used fertilizer and collected more than 48 tomatoes. I cannot believe how easily our harvest was *quadrupled!*

10. _____

For each word used incorrectly, write a sentence using the word properly.

_____

_____

_____

_____

_____

_____

_____

_____

_____

_____

_____

Bonus Words

The English language has many number prefixes. Most come from either Greek or Latin. Knowing these familiar prefixes will greatly increase your vocabulary.

Use Your Dictionary: Find as many words as you can that begin with one of these number prefixes. Write the words and a brief definition of each.

| bi- | di- | tri- |
| hepta- | penta- | |

Name _____

How well do you remember the words you studied in Lessons 7 through 9? Take the following test covering the words from the last three lessons.

Part 1 Antonyms

Each question below includes a word in capital letters, followed by four words or phrases. Choose the word or phrase that is most nearly <u>opposite</u> in meaning to the word in capital letters. Write the letter for your answer on the line provided.

Sample

| S. SLOW | (A) lazy | (B) simple | S. _____ |
| | (C) fast | (D) common | |

| 1. RILE | (A) churn | (B) divide | 1. _____ |
| | (C) argue | (D) soothe | |

| 2. SYNTHETIC | (A) cotton | (B) rare | 2. _____ |
| | (C) costly | (D) natural | |

| 3. FORSWEAR | (A) forgive | (B) support | 3. _____ |
| | (C) limit | (D) pray | |

| 4. MONARCHY | (A) poverty | (B) royalty | 4. _____ |
| | (C) democracy | (D) capitalism | |

| 5. LAMBASTE | (A) question | (B) praise | 5. _____ |
| | (C) apologize | (D) explain | |

| 6. IRREVERSIBLE | (A) changeable | (B) temporary | 6. _____ |
| | (C) permanent | (D) occasional | |

| 7. MONOTONOUS | (A) varied | (B) authoritative | 7. _____ |
| | (C) emotional | (D) strong | |

| 8. HARASS | (A) badger | (B) torment | 8. _____ |
| | (C) weaken | (D) comfort | |

| 9. UNIFORMITY | (A) complexity | (B) variety | 9. _____ |
| | (C) simplicity | (D) originality | |

| 10. BRUTISH | (A) quiet, shy | (B) lively, excited | 10. _____ |
| | (C) polite, civilized | (D) rude, inconsiderate | |

11. PRECISE	(A) measured	(B) inexact	11. _____
	(C) correct	(D) adequate	
12. THAW	(A) chill	(B) heat	12. _____
	(C) freeze	(D) cook	
13. QUADRUPLE	(A) divide by four	(B) provide	12. _____
	(C) honor	(D) clean	
14. INFILTRATE	(A) spy on	(B) repel	14. _____
	(C) recover	(D) overpower	
15. MUTILATE	(A) discover	(B) dispose of	15. _____
	(C) repair	(D) recognize	

Part 2 Matching Words and Meanings

Match the definition in Column B with the word in Column A. Write the letter of the correct definition on the line provided.

Column A	**Column B**	
16. meteorological	a. mock or insult	16. _____
17. skirmish	b. pierce, get through	17. _____
18. decathlon	c. nine days of prayer	18. _____
19. era	d. time period	19. _____
20. novena	e. battle or conflict	20. _____
21. penetrate	f. contest with 10 events	21. _____
22. sextet	g. imaginary line around the earth	22. _____
23. taunt	h. group of six	23. _____
24. hexagon	i. pertaining to the weather	24. _____
25. equator	j. figure with six sides	25. _____

Name _____

The Tale of Osebo's Drum
–an African Folktale

When Nyame the Sky God's mother died, he wanted her funeral to be one that would reflect the status of their family. He knew that the great drum of Osebo the Leopard would make the ceremony truly **regal**. Osebo was the most powerful animal on earth. He
5 would not willingly give up his great drum. Nyame **deliberated** for a long time, but he could not imagine a way to get the drum.

Nyame **convened** a meeting of all the animals and announced that he needed the great drum of Osebo for his mother's funeral. The animals **cowered** at the thought of challenging Osebo. Finally,
10 Elephant said he would try to get the drum, but he failed. Then Lion tried and failed. Antelope, Crocodile, and Bear could not get the drum either. When Turtle said, "I will get the drum," the other animals laughed hysterically. Turtle had a soft back, and moved as slowly as he does today. However, he was not at all **apprehensive**
15 about the challenge.

So, moving *very* slowly, Turtle finally arrived at Leopard's home. Osebo called out, "Have you come to try to steal my drum, too?"

"No," said Turtle, "but all this talk of drums has **piqued** my curiosity. I came to see just how great your drum is." When Osebo
20 showed Turtle his drum, Turtle **conceded** that, it was, indeed, a great drum. Then he said, "But Nyame's drum is larger. It is so large he can crawl inside it."

Osebo objected in a **ferocious** voice, claiming that his drum was certainly as large. To prove it, Osebo climbed inside. Once
25 Osebo was inside the drum, Turtle plugged its opening. He then tied the drum to his back and slowly dragged it back to Nyame. The animals were **flabbergasted** at Turtle's success.

Turtle presented the drum to Nyame with Osebo inside it. In exchange for his freedom, Osebo offered the drum to Nyame as
30 a gift. As he hurried away, Osebo stumbled into the Sky God's fire and **scorched** himself in many places, leaving dark spots on his hide. As a reward, Nyame offered Turtle anything he desired. Fearing the other animals, Turtle asked for a hard cover to protect his back. And to this day, the turtle always travels with a hard
35 shell on its back.

Words

apprehensive

concede

convene

cower

deliberate

ferocious

flabbergasted

pique

regal

scorch

Each word in this lesson's word list appears in dark type in the selection you just read. Think about how the vocabulary word is used in the selection. Then write the letter for the best answer to each question.

1. Another word for *regal* (line 4) is _____.
   (A) funny   (B) unpleasant
   (C) strange   (D) royal

   1. _____

2. *Deliberated* (line 5) means _____.
   (A) rested   (B) thought carefully
   (C) walked slowly   (D) demanded

   2. _____

3. If you *convene* (line 7) a meeting, you _____.
   (A) call it together   (B) end it suddenly
   (C) limit it   (D) cancel it

   3. _____

4. To *cower* (line 9) is to _____.
   (A) remain calm   (B) become enraged
   (C) shrink away in fear   (D) become bold and daring

   4. _____

5. Another word for *apprehensive* (line 14) is _____.
   (A) afraid   (B) helpful
   (C) amused   (D) informed

   5. _____

6. If you have *piqued* (line 18) someone's curiosity, you have _____ it.
   (A) reduced   (B) confused
   (C) excited   (D) satisfied

   6. _____

7. If you *concede* an idea (line 20), you _____.
   (A) brag about it   (B) acknowledge it as true
   (C) think it over carefully   (D) insist on its importance

   7. _____

8. A *ferocious* (line 23) voice is one that is _____.
   (A) difficult to hear   (B) filled with laughter
   (C) extremely fierce   (D) firm but gentle

   8. _____

9. Another word for *flabbergasted* (line 27) is _____.
   (A) astonished   (B) angered
   (C) resentful   (D) sad

   9. _____

10. Another word for *scorched* (line 31) is _____.
    (A) painted   (B) dried
    (C) scratched   (D) burned

  10. _____

Applying Meaning

Follow the directions below to write a sentence using a vocabulary word.

1. Describe a time when you had to make a decision. Use any form of the word *deliberate* in your sentence.

   _____

   _____

   _____

2. Write a sentence about an unexpected event. Use the word *flabbergasted*.

   _____

   _____

   _____

3. Write a sentence about something that happened at home. Use any form of the word *scorch* in your sentence.

   _____

   _____

   _____

4. Use the word *apprehensive* to describe someone faced with a new situation.

   _____

   _____

   _____

5. Describe a confrontation between two animals. Use any form of the word *cower*.

   _____

   _____

   _____

6. Write a sentence about two people settling a disagreement. Use any form of the word *concede*.

   _____

   _____

   _____

7. Describe someone who comes upon a locked chest. Use any form of the word *pique* in your sentence.

_____

_____

_____

8. Use the word *regal* in a sentence about power or authority.

_____

_____

_____

9. Use any form of the word *convene* to write a sentence about something that happened at school.

_____

_____

_____

10. Describe an animal using the word *ferocious*.

_____

_____

_____

Mastering Meaning

Folktales are often used to explain why something in nature is the way it is. "Osebo's Drum," for example, is a folktale from Ghana that tells why the turtle has a hard shell and why the leopard has spots. In most "why" stories the smaller, weaker animal is triumphant over the larger, more powerful animal. Choose an animal and write a short folktale that tells why that animal has a particular characteristic. You may want to write about why a pig has a curly tail, why an elephant has a long trunk, or why a lion has a mane. Try to use words from this lesson in your folktale.

Vocabulary of Quality and Worth

Name _____

Think of how boring descriptions would be if we were limited to using the adjectives *good* and *bad*. Even though these two words are not without meaning, they do not provide as precise or detailed a description of the value of things as other adjectives might. The English language has many adjectives that give a more exact description of the quality and worth of someone or something. In this lesson, you will learn 10 of these words.

Unlocking Meaning

Read the sentences or short passages below. Write the letter for the correct definition of the italicized vocabulary word.

1. For years, this farm produced rich crops, but now the soil is depleted of the nutrients needed for plant growth, and the fields are *barren*.
   (A) fiery
   (B) plentiful
   (C) dirty
   (D) unproductive

2. Mother urged me to copy my cousin's *exemplary* table manners. He never puts his elbows on the table, talks with his mouth full, or grabs for the food.
   (A) being a perfect example worth imitating
   (B) boring
   (C) having several points of view
   (D) puzzling or confusing

3. The museum guide pointed out the *exquisite* detail in the gold ornamentation around the base of the statue. I moved to get a closer look, wondering how the artist had sculpted the tiny, complicated designs.
   (A) plain and uncluttered
   (B) delicate and beautiful
   (C) repetitive
   (D) having no shape

4. I gasped when I saw the *extraordinary* size of Yoshi's prize-winning pumpkin. It was at least three feet wide!
   (A) plain and simple
   (B) moving at a rapid speed
   (C) beyond what is usual or expected
   (D) causing great confusion

5. Considering the seriousness of the discussion, the disagreement over where to go to lunch seemed *frivolous* and untimely.
   (A) emotional
   (B) argumentative
   (C) magical or mystical
   (D) unimportant

Words

barren

exemplary

exquisite

extraordinary

frivolous

inferior

marginal

petty

superb

trivial

1. _____

2. _____

3. _____

4. _____

5. _____

6. Recently, I purchased a less expensive brand of light bulbs. However, because of their *inferior* quality, they all burned out after only a few days of use.

(A) worse than others (B) aggravating
(C) enclosed or covered (D) repetitious

6. _____

7. Laura put only *marginal* effort into her science project. The project was accepted for the science fair, but Laura didn't receive an award.

(A) slippery or oily (B) quiet and timid
(C) barely good enough (D) talkative

7. _____

8. At the last meeting, we made a list of issues we needed to discuss. However, since the list was long, we decided to ignore the *petty* issues and concentrate on the important ones.

(A) attractive (B) unable to be measured
(C) insulting (D) lacking importance

8. _____

9. After the play, the cast received a standing ovation. Clearly, everyone in the audience felt it had been a *superb* show.

(A) excellent (B) abundant
(C) obvious (D) tiresome

9. _____

10. Luis's book report was filled with so many *trivial* details that it was difficult to determine exactly what he thought about the book.

(A) intellectual (B) insignificant
(C) uncertain (D) odd or unusual

10. _____

Name _____

Applying Meaning

Follow the directions below to write a sentence using a vocabulary word.

1. Use the word *superb* to describe an experience.

   _____

   _____

   _____

2. Write a sentence describing an article of clothing. Use the word *exquisite*.

   _____

   _____

   _____

3. Write a sentence about an area of land. Use the word *barren* in your sentence.

   _____

   _____

   _____

4. Use *inferior* in a sentence about something you own.

   _____

   _____

   _____

5. Use the word *extraordinary* to describe some recent weather.

   _____

   _____

   _____

Decide which word in parentheses best completes the sentence. Then write the sentence, adding the missing word.

6. Anita belongs to the Honor Society and tutors students after school. That's why she is considered a(n) _____ student. (trivial; exemplary)

   _____

   _____

   _____

7. The final exam grade is no _____ matter. (trivial; superb)

_____

_____

_____

8. The principal ignored the _____ complaints about the lockers and addressed only important questions. (exemplary; petty)

_____

_____

_____

9. Jerry had only _____ musical talent, but through hard work he learned to play the guitar quite well. (barren; marginal)

_____

_____

_____

10. I watch only quality TV. I think sit coms and made-for-TV movies are _____. (frivolous; exemplary)

_____

_____

_____

Cultural Literacy Note

Nero's Fiddle

Legend has it that while ancient Rome was burning, Emperor Nero stood by and played his violin, apparently undisturbed by the massive destruction occurring around him. The expression "fiddling while Rome burns" is often used to describe people who carry on in a frivolous and carefree manner while problems continue to mount around them.

Write a Paragraph: Have you ever been frustrated by someone who ignored something important because he or she was more concerned with trivial matters? Have you ever done something frivolous and ignored an urgent problem? Write a paragraph describing an instance when you or someone else "fiddled while Rome burned." Use some of the words you studied in this lesson.

The Prefix de-

Name _____

The prefix *de-* appears at the beginning of a large number of English words. Although it has several meanings, its most common meanings are "to reverse" or "to reduce." This prefix comes from the Latin preposition *de*, meaning "down" or "away from." All the words in this lesson begin with the prefix *de-*.

Unlocking Meaning

Words

- deface
- defective
- defer
- deformity
- degrade
- dehydrate
- denounce
- deplete
- deprive
- deterrent

Write a vocabulary word for each of these definitions or clues. Then rewrite the definition in your own words. Use the dictionary in the back of the book to check your answer.

1. The Latin root *plere*, meaning "to fill" is seen in this word. You might do this to your supply of water in the desert.

   _____

   _____

   _____

2. This verb comes from *deferre*, a Latin word meaning "to carry or put off."

   _____

   _____

   _____

3. A form of the word *deter*, this three-syllable word comes from the Latin word meaning "to frighten."

   _____

   _____

   _____

4. The word *form* can be found in this word. Pollution can cause this in fish.

   _____

   _____

   _____

5. Its literal meaning might be "to go down a grade," but it does not mean to repeat a grade in school.

_____

_____

_____

6. One example of this action might be drawing a mustache on a picture of someone you do not like.

_____

_____

_____

7. The Greek word part *hydro*, meaning "water," can be seen in this verb.

_____

_____

_____

8. This adjective might describe a clock that does not keep time or a pipe that leaks.

_____

_____

_____

9. This word combines the *de-* prefix with the Latin word *nuntiare*, meaning "to announce." If it is about you, it is an announcement you would rather not hear.

_____

_____

_____

10. This word includes the Latin word *privare*, meaning "to rob." It might refer to wealth or opportunity.

_____

_____

_____

Applying Meaning

Decide which word in parentheses best completes the sentence. Then write the sentence, adding the missing word.

1. Vandals _____ the front of our school building with spray-painted graffiti. (defaced; deprived)

_____

_____

_____

2. The _____ of the puppy's leg was caused by a traffic accident. (deformity; deterrent)

_____

_____

_____

3. This appliance will _____ any type of fruit. (deface; dehydrate)

_____

_____

_____

4. The candidate refused to _____ herself by accepting the gangster's money. (deprive; degrade)

_____

_____

_____

5. I return library books on time because I don't want to _____ anyone else of the opportunity to read them. (defer; deprive)

_____

_____

_____

Read each sentence below. Write "correct" on the answer line if the vocabulary word has been used correctly or "incorrect" if it has been used incorrectly.

6. I had mistakenly concluded that my new watch was *defective* when, in fact, it just needed a new battery.

6. _____

7. This *deterrent* is guaranteed to remove stains from all types of fabrics.

7. _____

8. As I entered the ballroom, the butler loudly *denounced* my arrival. I felt like some kind of royalty.

8. _____

9. If we do not develop new ways of creating energy, we will eventually *deplete* our fuel supply.

9. _____

10. Look closely at the slides under the microscope, and you will see how each type of bacteria *defers* from the others.

10. _____

For each word used incorrectly, write a sentence using the word correctly.

_____

_____

_____

_____

_____

_____

Test-Taking Strategies

Some tests assess your knowledge of standard English grammar and usage. These tests usually show you a sentence with four underlined parts and ask you to write the letter of the underlined part that contains an error. Read the entire sentence before choosing your answer. Look carefully at each choice. When you think you have found the error, ask yourself how you would correct it. There will never be more than one error.

Practice: Write the letter for the underlined part of the sentence that has an error. If there is no error, write E.

1. Walking through the theater, Jim and her asked everyone in
           A   B
attendance to keep his or her seat while the sound system
                        C
was being repaired. No Error
        D   E

1. _____

2. Since my conversation with Jane was just between her and me, I
                                                A   B
shut my door so my brothers could not listen to us. No Error
                        C   D   E

2. _____

3. Our teacher told each member of the class to remember to bring
                        A   B
their permission slip for the field trip on Friday. No Error
C   D   E

3. _____

Name _____

How well do you remember the words you studied in Lessons 10 through 12? Take the following test covering the words from the last three lessons.

Part 1 Choose the Correct Meaning

Each question below includes a word in capital letters, followed by four words or phrases. Choose the word or phrase that is <u>closest</u> in meaning to the word in capital letters. Write the letter for your answer on the line provided.

Sample

S. FINISH	(A) enjoy (C) destroy	(B) complete (D) enlarge	S. _____

1. EXTRAORDINARY	(A) great (C) supernatural	(B) very ordinary (D) uncommon	1. _____
2. DEFECTIVE	(A) foreign (C) imperfect	(B) criminal (D) hard	2. _____
3. DEPLETE	(A) save (C) use up	(B) transport (D) pack	3. _____
4. SUPERB	(A) outstanding (C) well-known	(B) committed (D) tough	4. _____
5. PIQUE	(A) measure (C) select	(B) stir (D) renew	5. _____
6. DEHYDRATE	(A) dry out (C) spoil	(B) forget (D) care for	6. _____
7. SCORCH	(A) scrape (C) burn	(B) tempt (D) release	7. _____
8. FEROCIOUS	(A) nervous (C) fierce	(B) gentle (D) confined	8. _____
9. EXEMPLARY	(A) excused (C) tough	(B) unbelievable (D) model	9. _____
10. CONCEDE	(A) reverse (C) remove	(B) declare (D) acknowledge	10. _____

11. TRIVIAL   (A) difficult   (B) unimportant   11. _____
                (C) silly   (D) repeated

12. MARGINAL   (A) just enough   (B) branded   12. _____
                (C) flimsy   (D) poor

13. REGAL   (A) legal   (B) royal   13. _____
                (C) powerful   (D) well-known

14. BARREN   (A) green   (B) dry   14. _____
                (C) unproductive   (D) hilly

15. DEFER   (A) delay   (B) repeat   15. _____
                (C) explore   (D) deny

Part 2 Matching Words and Meanings

Match the definition in Column B with the word in Column A. Write the letter of the correct definition on the line provided.

Column A	Column B	
16. apprehensive	a. overcome with amazement	16. _____
17. inferior	b. very beautiful	17. _____
18. cower	c. lower in rank or quality	18. _____
19. deface	d. to blame	19. _____
20. deformity	e. to hide in fear	20. _____
21. exquisite	f. to bring together	21. _____
22. deterrent	g. something that discourages	22. _____
23. convene	h. fearful or uneasy	23. _____
24. flabbergasted	i. disfigurement	24. _____
25. denounce	j. to damage	25. _____

Name _____

Harriet Tubman

Born a slave in Maryland around the year 1815, Harriet Tubman was forced to work as a field hand by her cruel plantation overseer. In 1849, Tubman fled the plantation, leaving behind her husband, her parents, and her brothers and sisters. Tubman was driven by her
5 belief that all African Americans should be free. Her **unequivocal** dedication to this cause never **wavered**. Risking her life as well as her freedom, she returned to the South no fewer than 19 times to lead her family and hundreds of other slaves to freedom. Tubman guided the escaping slaves north along the Underground Railroad, a
10 secret organization that aided the escape of slaves to Canada. None of the fugitives Harriet Tubman led to safety was ever captured. All the while, Tubman herself was **pursued** by bounty hunters who sought the 40 thousand dollars offered for her capture.

Tubman later **conspired** with John Brown when he planned his
15 attack on Harper's Ferry in 1858. She provided valuable information that helped him carry out his raid. She even planned to participate in the raid but was ill at the time. When the Civil War broke out three years later, Tubman assisted the Union Army as a nurse and served as both a scout and a spy. Her knowledge of the land, her
20 experience at secret travel, and her **unremarkable** looks allowed her to carry out her duties without being spotted. She was so important to the Union Army, in fact, that she was a leader of a corps of local blacks who **ventured** into rebel territory to gather information. Because she was **privy** to information on the location of ware-
25 houses and ammunition depots, she was able to provide **vital** information to Union commanders. Her information helped Colonel James Montgomery make several **expeditions** into southern areas to destroy supplies.

After the war, Tubman returned to New York, where, while car-
30 ing for her own family, she helped escaped and newly freed blacks begin their lives. She earned money by giving speeches and selling copies of her biography. In 1896, she was the oldest member present for the organizational meeting of the National Association of Colored Women. Called "the Moses of her people," Tubman came
35 to **personify** the strength and determination that eventually led to the civil rights movement of the 1960s.

Words
conspire
expedition
personify
privy
pursue
unequivocal
unremarkable
venture
vital
waver

Each word in this lesson's word list appears in dark type in the selection you just read. Think about how the vocabulary word is used in the selection. Then write the letter for the best answer to each question.

1. An *unequivocal* (line 5) dedication _____.   1. _____
   (A) lacks sincerity   (B) is superior to all others
   (C) has no doubts   (D) might change at any time

2. Another word for *wavered* (line 6), is _____.   2. _____
   (A) showed   (B) increased
   (C) changed   (D) listened

3. Another word for *pursued* (line 12) is _____.   3. _____
   (A) requested   (B) squeezed
   (C) thanked   (D) chased

4. If you *conspire* (line 14) with someone, you _____ with him or her.   4. _____
   (A) plot   (B) argue
   (C) travel   (D) share a meal

5. If something is *unremarkable* (line 20), it is _____.   5. _____
   (A) ordinary   (B) valuable
   (C) complicated   (D) full of meaning

6. To *venture* (line 23) is to _____.   6. _____
   (A) refuse assistance   (B) make a daring journey
   (C) observe closely   (D) avoid

7. If you are *privy* (line 24) to information, you _____.   7. _____
   (A) are unaware of it   (B) are confused by it
   (C) are embarrassed by it   (D) have secret knowledge of it

8. Which word could best replace *vital* in line 25?   8. _____
   (A) incorrect   (B) unfamiliar
   (C) essential   (D) popular

9. An *expedition* (line 27) is a(n) _____.   9. _____
   (A) noisy display   (B) excursion
   (C) expectation   (D) betrayal

10. To *personify* (line 35) something means to _____.   10. _____
    (A) serve as an example of it   (B) make fun of it
    (C) object to it   (D) misunderstand it

Applying Meaning

Decide which word in parentheses best completes the sentence. Then write the sentence, adding the missing word.

1. Eating well and getting plenty of exercise are _____ to good health. (unremarkable; vital)

   _____

   _____

   _____

2. Since everyone passed the state mathematics test easily, the principal called the results a(n) _____ success. (privy; unequivocal)

   _____

   _____

   _____

3. The police had to _____ the thief on foot for blocks before they were able to catch her. (personify; pursue)

   _____

   _____

   _____

4. My sister and I _____ for weeks to give our brother a great surprise birthday party. (conspired; wavered)

   _____

   _____

   _____

5. After I got lost taking a walk through the forest, I never again _____ into the woods alone. (ventured; conspired)

   _____

   _____

   _____

6. The teachers found it difficult to prepare us for the entrance exam since they were not _____ to the questions. (privy; vital)

   _____

   _____

   _____

7. With her gentle nature, constant smile, and unending generosity, Julie _____ kindness. (personifies; wavers)

_____

_____

_____

8. The candidates debated the tax issue for hours, but neither politician _____ from his original position. (wavered; pursued)

_____

_____

_____

9. As the most experienced diver in the group, Ken was chosen to lead the _____ into the underwater caves. (expedition; privy)

_____

_____

_____

10. We found it hard to believe that a millionaire lived in such a(n) _____ home. (unremarkable; vital)

_____

_____

_____

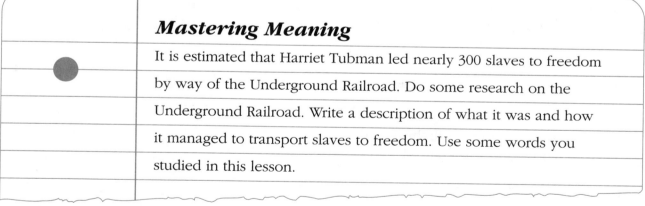

Mastering Meaning

It is estimated that Harriet Tubman led nearly 300 slaves to freedom by way of the Underground Railroad. Do some research on the Underground Railroad. Write a description of what it was and how it managed to transport slaves to freedom. Use some words you studied in this lesson.

Confusing Words

Name _____

Some words in the English language look and sound like other words. However, their meanings may be quite different. This can lead to confusion. Therefore, knowing the meaning of these words will ensure that you use them correctly. In this lesson, you will learn four sets of similar words. Each word in a set has a different meaning.

Unlocking Meaning

Read the sentences or short passages below. Write the letter for the correct definition of the italicized vocabulary word.

1. As we rounded the bend in the road I caught *sight* of deer grazing in a field.
   (A) to quote or mention as proof
   (B) a place where something is or will be located
   (C) the act of seeing

2. A monument stands on the *site* where Abraham Lincoln delivered his famous Gettysburg Address.
   (A) to quote or mention as proof
   (B) a place where something is or will be located
   (C) the act of seeing

3. To prove her point, the governor was able to *cite* several key facts without having to check her notes.
   (A) to quote or mention as proof
   (B) a place where something is or will be located
   (C) the act of seeing

4. We painted the room white and put mirrors on all the walls to create the *illusion* of a larger room.
   (A) an indirect reference
   (B) an unreal or misleading appearance

5. John's remark about not being his brother's keeper was an *allusion* to the biblical story of Cain and Abel.
   (A) an indirect reference
   (B) an unreal or misleading appearance

Words

- **adapt**
- **adept**
- **adopt**
- **allusion**
- **illusion**
- **cite**
- **sight**
- **site**
- **complement**
- **compliment**

1. _____

2. _____

3. _____

4. _____

5. _____

6. Your grades might improve if you *adopt* some of the study habits
suggested by the counselor.
(A) adjust or modify
(B) thoroughly skilled
(C) accept or take as one's own

6. _____

7. When our grandfather came to live with us, I had to *adapt* to
sharing my room with another person.
(A) adjust or modify
(B) thoroughly skilled
(C) accept or take as one's own

7. _____

8. Although he had never used a computer before, Mark has become
quite *adept* at sending e-mail and using the word processor.
(A) adjust or modify
(B) thoroughly skilled
(C) accept or take as one's own

8. _____

9. The rich dessert was the perfect *complement* to the delicious
dinner we'd just eaten.
(A) something that completes or makes whole
(B) an expression of praise

9. _____

10. My mother is hardworking and responsible. Whenever anyone
says that I am like her, I take it as a great *compliment*.
(A) something that completes or makes whole
(B) an expression of praise

10. _____

Applying Meaning

Decide which word in parentheses best completes the sentence. Then write the sentence, adding the missing word.

1. The plaque says this is the _____ of the Boston Massacre. (cite; site)

    _____

    _____

    _____

2. I was flattered when I heard a respected artist _____ my painting. (complementing; complimenting)

    _____

    _____

    _____

3. The professional figure skater is so _____ that she makes complicated maneuvers on the ice look simple. (adapt; adept)

    _____

    _____

    _____

4. My cousin agreed to wear a bright yellow jacket so I would be able to identify her the moment she came into _____. (sight; site)

    _____

    _____

    _____

5. The scenery was designed with care to create the _____ that the actors were inside a deep cave. (allusion; illusion)

    _____

    _____

    _____

6. When the soccer team needed new uniforms, they decided to _____ the choir's fund-raising strategy and hold a bake sale. (adept; adopt)

    _____

    _____

    _____

7. Our new puppy quickly _____ to her new home. (adapted; adopted)

_____

_____

_____

8. Lovers are often referred to as Romeo or Juliet, an _____ to the play by Shakespeare. (allusion; illusion)

_____

_____

_____

9. When asked to explain why we needed a new library, the mayor _____ many reasons why the old building was inadequate. (cited; sited)

_____

_____

_____

10. Before I left for the party, my sister gave me a stuffed mouse, saying it was the perfect _____ to my cat costume. (complement; compliment)

_____

_____

_____

Spelling and Meaning

Dropping a Final *e* Before Adding *-ed* or *-ing*

You can simply add *-ed* or *-ing* to most words. However, when a word ends with *e*, the final *e* is dropped before adding *-ed* or *-ing*.

cite   citing   cited

Practice the Strategy: Add *-ed* and *-ing* to each of these words.

announce	cure	describe	jump	destroy
invite	plead	provide	slice	trace

Adjective Suffixes

Name _____

The suffixes *-ent*, *-ous*, and *-ose* signal a reader that the words they are attached to are adjectives. Adjectives are words that describe nouns or pronouns. In this lesson, you will learn 10 adjectives with these suffixes. Knowing these adjectives can help you provide accurate, vivid descriptions of people, places, or things when you speak and write.

Unlocking Meaning

A vocabulary word appears in italics in each sentence or short passage below. Note the adjective suffix in the word and think about how the word is used in the passage. Then write a definition for the vocabulary word. Compare your definition with the definition in the dictionary at the back of the book.

Words
corpulent
fraudulent
hilarious
luminous
morose
prosperous
treacherous
turbulent
verbose
wondrous

1. The clothing store began to carry a variety of clothes in larger sizes to accommodate their many *corpulent* customers.

   _____

   _____

   _____

2. The men were accused of creating a *fraudulent* charity to collect thousands of dollars from trusting contributors.

   _____

   _____

   _____

3. Harry's *hilarious* story about the fishing trip made us laugh until tears were rolling down our cheeks.

   _____

   _____

   _____

4. Thanks to the *luminous* full moon, we were able to watch the raccoon leave the forest in search of food.

   _____

   _____

   _____

5. The last-minute loss to our archrivals caused a *morose* stillness in the once noisy football stadium.

_____

_____

_____

6. It took years of hard work by the new owner to turn the failed laundry into a *prosperous* business.

_____

_____

_____

7. The mountain climbers moved slowly up the *treacherous* edge of a narrow ridge leading to the summit.

_____

_____

_____

8. As the raft entered the *turbulent* waters of the raging river, the guide advised everyone to check his or her life preserver.

_____

_____

_____

9. Unlike the *verbose* speech of Edward Everett, Lincoln's Gettysburg Address took only a few minutes to deliver.

_____

_____

_____

10. The many *wondrous* inventions attributed to Thomas Edison are a source of amazement to modern historians.

_____

_____

_____

Name _____

Applying Meaning

Follow the directions below to write a sentence using a vocabulary word.

1. Use *turbulent* in a sentence about something in nature.

   _____

   _____

   _____

2. Write a sentence about a period of American history. Use the word *prosperous*.

   _____

   _____

   _____

3. Write a sentence about someone's mood. Use the word *morose*.

   _____

   _____

   _____

4. Describe a scheme to do something illegal. Use *fraudulent*.

   _____

   _____

   _____

5. Write a sentence about something that happened at night. Use the word *luminous* in your sentence.

   _____

   _____

   _____

Each question contains a vocabulary word from this lesson. Answer each question "yes" or "no" in the space provided.

6. If a buyer were willing to pay by the pound, would a farmer prefer to sell a *corpulent* pig?

6. _____

7. Is a field full of hills considered *hilarious*?

7. _____

8. Is driving on an icy road on a stormy night *treacherous*?

8. _____

9. Is a test on the parts of speech a test of *verbose* ability?

9. _____

10. Would you expect a superhero to perform *wondrous* and heroic feats?

10. _____

For each question you answered "no," write a sentence explaining
your reason.

_____

_____

_____

_____

_____

_____

_____

_____

_____

Bonus Word

infamous

It would be reasonable for someone to assume that the adjective
infamous describes someone or something that is not famous, since
the *in-* prefix usually means "not." *Infamous*, however, is used to
describe someone or something that is, in fact, widely known. While
famous refers to someone or something that is well known for positive
reasons, *infamous* usually has negative connotations. For example,
criminals or scandals are frequently described as *infamous*. There are
other English words that begin with the *in-* prefix in which *in-* does
not mean "not."

Use Your Dictionary: Find the following words in a dictionary. Write a
definition for the word, then write a sentence, using the word correctly.

inflammable   invaluable   ingenious   ingenuous

Name _____

How well do you remember the words you studied in Lessons 13 through 15? Take the following test covering the words from the last three lessons.

Part 1 Choose the Correct Meaning

Each question below includes a word in capital letters, followed by four words or phrases. Choose the word or phrase that is <u>closest</u> in meaning to the word in capital letters. Write the letter for your answer on the line provided.

Sample

S. FINISH	(A) enjoy	(B) complete	S. _____
	(C) destroy	(D) enlarge	

1. FRAUDULENT	(A) dishonest	(B) cheap	1. _____
	(C) copied	(D) firm	

2. UNREMARKABLE	(A) ordinary	(B) silent	2. _____
	(C) single	(D) tragic	

3. CITE	(A) reward	(B) scold	3. _____
	(C) copy	(D) quote	

4. VITAL	(A) long	(B) necessary	4. _____
	(C) extra	(D) expensive	

5. CORPULENT	(A) ugly	(B) well-dressed	5. _____
	(C) fat	(D) unhealthy	

6. ALLUSION	(A) falseness	(B) reference	6. _____
	(C) comparison	(D) interpretation	

7. VERBOSE	(A) lively	(B) wordy	7. _____
	(C) worried	(D) green	

8. ADEPT	(A) skilled	(B) adjust	8. _____
	(C) unsure	(D) slow	

9. COMPLIMENT	(A) complete	(B) limit	9. _____
	(C) record	(D) praise	

10. PURSUE	(A) carry	(B) charge	10. _____
	(C) chase	(D) review	

11. ADAPT   (A) skilled   (B) adjust   11. _____

                 (C) unsure   (D) slow

12. ILLUSION   (A) deception   (B) reference   12. _____

                 (C) comparison   (D) interpretation

13. COMPLEMENT   (A) complete   (B) limit   13. _____

                 (C) record   (D) praise

14. CONSPIRE   (A) raise   (B) plot   14. _____

                 (C) decorate   (D) steal

15. MOROSE   (A) stupid   (B) forgotten   15. _____

                 (C) gloomy   (D) red

Part 2 Matching Words and Meanings

Match the definition in Column B with the word in Column A. Write the letter of the correct definition on the line provided.

Column A	Column B	
16. sight	a. very funny	16. _____
17. site	b. vision	17. _____
18. hilarious	c. wealthy	18. _____
19. wondrous	d. embody or represent	19. _____
20. personify	e. make a daring undertaking	20. _____
21. waver	f. hesitate or change	21. _____
22. adopt	g. take in or assume	22. _____
23. prosperous	h. place	23. _____
24. luminous	i. bright	24. _____
25. venture	j. amazing	25. _____

Lesson
16
Part A

Name _____

Giganotosaurus

For many years, **paleontologists** thought that the *Tyrannosaurus rex* was the largest meat-eating dinosaur ever to roam the earth. In 1995, however, an auto mechanic and **amateur** scientist named Ruben Carolini discovered some
5   bones in Argentina. This discovery was to **unseat** *Tyrannosaurus rex* from its position as the largest meat-eating dinosaur. In honor of his discovery, scientists named the new dinosaur *Gigantosaurus Carolini*.

   After the initial find, scientists **exhumed** additional pieces
10 of the *Gigantosaurus's* skeleton. They found parts of the skull, many of the vertebrae, both thigh bones, and some teeth. Each of the curved teeth was eight inches long and **serrated** like a saw. From this incomplete skeleton, scientists were able to **estimate** the dinosaur's size and appearance.

15   According to researchers, the *Gigantosaurus* was about 42 feet long, making it slightly longer that the *Tyrannosaurus rex*. The creature ran on its hind legs and had rather small arms. It weighed six to eight tons, making it nearly three tons heavier than the largest *Tyrannosaurus rex*.

   Scientists do not know exactly what the *Gigantosaurus* ate,
20 but its teeth have all the **attributes** of meat-eating animals, so they have concluded that the great beast was a carnivore, or meat eater.

   Because skeletal remains of dinosaurs do not include skin, scientists must **theorize** about the dinosaurs' skin
25 colors. A *Gigantosaurus* hunted smaller **prey,** so it is likely that the appearance of its skin allowed it to blend into its surroundings in order to surprise its victims. The *Gigantosaurus* lived in the grassy wetlands of what is now Argentina, an environment similar to the African savanna.
30 Therefore, this dinosaur probably had skin that closely matched the colors of the **vegetation** around it.

   The *Gigantosaurus Carolini* lived about 100 million years ago, some 30 million years before the *Tyrannosaurus rex* that roamed North America. Despite many similarities between
35 the two creatures, scientists have stated that the two are not closely related and that each species developed independently.

Words

amateur

attribute

estimate

exhume

paleontologist

prey

serrated

theorize

unseat

vegetation

Each word in this lesson's word list appears in dark type in the selection you just read. Think about how the vocabulary word is used in the selection. Then write the letter for the best answer to each question.

1. A *paleontologist* (line 1) studies _____.
   (A) fossils and prehistoric forms of life
   (B) medieval customs
   (C) volcanoes
   (D) distant galaxies

   1. _____

2. An *amateur* (line 3) scientist is one who is _____.
   (A) very athletic
   (B) highly paid
   (C) skillful
   (D) not a professional

   2. _____

3. If something is *unseated* (line 5), it is _____.
   (A) angered
   (B) removed from its position
   (C) lifted up
   (D) made to wait for a long while

   3. _____

4. If something is *exhumed* (line 8), it is _____.
   (A) thrown away
   (B) donated to science
   (C) taken from its grave
   (D) destroyed by fire

   4. _____

5. A *serrated* (line 11) tooth _____.
   (A) is cracked and broken
   (B) has a smooth surface
   (C) has begun to decay
   (D) has jagged, sharp edges

   5. _____

6. Which word could best replace *estimate* in line 12?
   (A) guess
   (B) enjoy
   (C) forget
   (D) dislike

   6. _____

7. Another word for *attributes* (line 20) is _____.
   (A) length
   (B) characteristics
   (C) gifts
   (D) color

   7. _____

8. If you *theorize* (line 23), you _____.
   (A) make an assumption based on available facts
   (B) argue at great length
   (C) prove beyond a doubt
   (D) prohibit something from being discussed publicly

   8. _____

9. *Prey* (line 25) is a(n) _____.
   (A) religious activity
   (B) type of tree
   (C) animal hunted for food
   (D) place to rest

   9. _____

10. Which word or phrase could best replace *vegetation* in line 30?
    (A) flightless birds
    (B) conflict
    (C) emotions
    (D) plant life

    10. _____

Applying Meaning

Decide which word in parentheses best completes the sentence. Then write the sentence, adding the missing word.

1. The court gave permission to _____ the body of the victim in order to search for more evidence of a crime. (estimate; exhume)

_____

_____

_____

2. Jamie is fascinated by _____; she spends all her time reading about dinosaurs and other prehistoric creatures. (paleontology; vegetation)

_____

_____

_____

3. My brother won the chess match and _____ the champion who had won the previous three years. (estimated; unseated)

_____

_____

_____

4. Even though the whale has many of the _____ of a fish, it is actually a mammal. (attributes; prey)

_____

_____

_____

5. The doctor _____ that a combination of the heat and a lack of fluids caused Fran to faint. (theorized; serrated)

_____

_____

_____

Read each sentence below. Write "correct" on the answer line if the vocabulary word has been used correctly or "incorrect" if it has been used incorrectly.

6. When Maria realized she was being *serrated*, she went to her window to listen to the singing.

6. _____

7. I don't know exactly how many pennies are in this jar, but I *estimate*
that there are about five hundred of them.

7. _____

8. After he threw the temper tantrum, I told my brother to quit acting
like such an *amateur*.

8. _____

9. The lion stalked its *prey* for hours before attacking it at the watering
hole.

9. _____

10. My cousin recently decided to become a *vegetation*. She stopped
eating any meat.

10. _____

For each word used incorrectly, write a sentence using the word properly.

_____

_____

_____

_____

_____

_____

_____

_____

_____

_____

_____

Mastering Meaning

Dinosaurs continue to capture the imagination of scientists and non-scientists alike. Everything from movies to museum exhibits about dinosaurs continues to be very popular attractions. Some dinosaurs ate plants, others ate animals. Some were small, others huge. Some flew, and one type even had a bill like that of a duck. Choose one type of dinosaur and prepare a report. Describe its size, shape, diet, and any other characteristics of interest. Include a picture if possible. Use words you studied in this lesson.

Vocabulary of Literature

Name _____

Writers use words to communicate ideas and images to readers. Literature is the artistic arrangement of words into poems, stories, plays, and books. In this lesson, you will learn 10 words associated with literature and the literary techniques that writers use.

Unlocking Meaning

Read the sentences or short passages below. Write the letter for the correct definition of the italicized vocabulary word.

Words
anthology
epic
epigram
fable
foreshadow
pun
sonnet
stanza
symbolism
tragedy

1. The *anthology* of African literature that Ms. Rogers gave me included several of my favorite short stories and poems.
   (A) discussion or argument on a specific topic
   (B) stories about war
   (C) collection of literary works
   (D) store where books and magazines are sold

2. In the first part of *Beowulf,* the great English *epic*, Beowulf defeats the monster Grendel. In the final part, he slays a fire-breathing dragon but is himself mortally wounded.
   (A) story about a legendary superhero
   (B) poem that mourns the death of a person
   (C) words of praise
   (D) type of rhyme

3. Oscar Wilde, known as the master of the *epigram*, once said, "What is a cynic? A man who knows the price of everything and the value of nothing."
   (A) type of print press
   (B) brief, witty comment
   (C) role model
   (D) the origin and history of a word

4. We discussed the moral of the *fable* about the tortoise and the hare.
   (A) story that gives a true description of animals
   (B) story with animal characters that teaches a lesson
   (C) humorous short story
   (D) any story about turtles and rabbits

5. The raging storm, the eerie castle, and the howling dog all seemed to *foreshadow* the mysterious disappearance.
   (A) hint of past events in a story
   (B) hide from the reader
   (C) mislead a reader about
   (D) provide clues to what will occur later

1. _____

2. _____

3. _____

4. _____

5. _____

6. When the new hair salon chose the name "Curl Up and Dye,"
   I knew the owners enjoyed a clever *pun*.
   (A) long, humorous story   (B) final thought on a subject
   (C) humor resulting from the   (D) bitter remark
        similarity of words

6. _____

7. The length and rhyming pattern of a Shakespearean *sonnet* is
   exactly defined.
   (A) story about an event from   (B) story about the adventures
        history   of the gods
   (C) long speech given by a   (D) type of poem
        character in a play

7. _____

8. Poe's poem "The Raven" is divided into 18 *stanzas*; the last 11 end
   with the word "nevermore."
   (A) group of lines in a poem   (B) single line of verse
   (C) first two lines of a poem   (D) parts of a poem with no
                                         regular pattern

8. _____

9. I could not understand the *symbolism* of the bird in the story until
   Ms. Romero suggested that the great white bird might stand for
   the secrets and treasures of nature.
   (A) detailed description   (B) surprise ending
   (C) using something to stand   (D) hidden thoughts of a story
        for something else   character

9. _____

10. At the end of *Hamlet,* a well-known Shakespearean *tragedy,* all the
    central characters, including Hamlet, die from poison.
    (A) play set in a small village   (B) dramatic reading
    (C) play in which the characters   (D) serious drama in which the
         encounter a series of comic   main character meets with
         mishaps   misfortune

10. _____

Applying Meaning

Decide which word in parentheses best completes the sentence. Then write the sentence, adding the missing word.

1. Enrique's joke was nothing but a silly _____ about a poor skunk who did not have a scent to his name. (anthology; pun)

   _____

   _____

   _____

2. Homer's *Iliad* is the classic _____ of Achilles, the legendary hero of Greece. (epic; epigram)

   _____

   _____

   _____

3. I could not understand all of the _____ in the story, although I did figure out that the book of fairy tales stood for the innocence of youth. (symbolism; tragedy)

   _____

   _____

   _____

4. The book of poems included both long narrative poems and some _____. (fables; sonnets)

   _____

   _____

   _____

5. I like the _____ "I can resist everything but temptation." (epic; epigram)

   _____

   _____

   _____

6. Aesop's _____ about the fox and the grapes gave us the expression "sour grapes." (fable; stanza)

   _____

   _____

   _____

Each question below contains one or more vocabulary words from this lesson. Answer each question "yes" or "no" in the space provided.

7. Might a student of literature buy a large *anthology* of her favorite writers?

7. _____

8. Would an *epigram* consist of several *stanzas*?

8. _____

9. Could the discovery of a bloody flag *foreshadow* a *tragedy* in a kingdom?

9. _____

10. Is an *epigram* an essay about an *epic*?

10. _____

For each question you answered "no," write a sentence explaining your reason.

_____

_____

_____

_____

_____

_____

_____

	Bonus Word
●	**cliché**
	Just as *epigram* refers to a short, clever statement, *cliché* refers to an
	empty, overused expression. The word came into English from the
	French word *clicher*, meaning "click." It was first used to refer to a
	printing plate called a stereotype because it made a clicking sound
	when type was produced. Since the *cliché* printed the same thing over
	and over, *cliché* came to mean any overused or overworked expression
	that has lost its meaning. Good writers avoid using *clichés* such as
	"pretty as a picture," "slept like a log," and "sly as a fox."
	Rewrite a Cliché: Make a list of at least five clichés. Then rewrite them
	to make them fresh and meaningful. What other comparison might be
	used to describe how sly someone is or how well you slept?

Noun Suffixes

Name _____

The suffixes *-ance, -ence, -ancy,* and *-ency* form nouns from adjectives or verbs. Sometimes you can simply add the suffix to a word. For example, the verb *repent* becomes the noun *repentance*. Other words, such as *convenient*, require that you change the spelling when the suffix is added. In this lesson, you will learn 10 words that have these noun suffixes.

Unlocking Meaning

Write the vocabulary word that best fits each clue below. Then write a short definition. Compare your definition with the one in the dictionary at the back of the book.

1. This noun is formed from the verb *depend*. It comes from the Latin word *dependere*, meaning "to hang down or against."

   _____

   _____

   _____

2. It rhymes with the word *emergency* and has a similar meaning.

   _____

   _____

   _____

3. It is formed from the verb *repent* and the *-ance* noun suffix.

   _____

   _____

   _____

4. You see the word *extra* in this word. A large diamond ring or an expensive sports car might be examples.

   _____

   _____

   _____

Words

consistency
convenience
dependency
extravagance
proficiency
repentance
resistance
truancy
urgency
vagrancy

5. This word combines the Latin *com-* meaning "together" and *venire* meaning "come." It makes life a little easier.

_____

_____

_____

6. This word comes from the Latin prefix *re-* meaning "back" and the Latin verb *sistere* meaning "to place." Citizens of a country might offer this to invaders.

_____

_____

_____

7. The Latin word *vagari* means "to wander." This noun stands for one type of wandering.

_____

_____

_____

8. It is formed from the word *truant*. In Middle English a truant was a beggar. If you're not in school, maybe you're out begging.

_____

_____

_____

9. This word comes from the Latin word *consistere* meaning "to stand still." It is something you look for in a friend or supporter.

_____

_____

_____

10. It's a synonym for *competence*. When you spend a long time mastering a language, a science, or an art, it leads to this.

_____

_____

_____

Applying Meaning

Decide which word in parentheses best completes the sentence. Then write the sentence, adding the missing word.

1. When calling for help in an emergency, always advise the operator of the _____ of the situation. (proficiency; urgency)

   _____

   _____

   _____

2. It took years of training to reach the level of _____ she has attained in medicine. (dependency; proficiency)

   _____

   _____

   _____

3. Given her limited budget, Pat could ill afford the _____ of a new car every year. (extravagance; convenience)

   _____

   _____

   _____

4. After moving to the suburbs, I began to appreciate the _____ of walking to stores and movies. (extravagance; convenience)

   _____

   _____

   _____

5. After two atomic bombs were dropped on their cities, the Japanese offered no more _____ and surrendered. (resistance; truancy)

   _____

   _____

   _____

6. Before Jesse was able to overcome his _____ on his parents, he had to get a job and his own apartment. (dependency; resistance)

   _____

   _____

   _____

7. Since the prisoner showed no sign of _____ for her crimes, the board turned down her request for a reduced sentence. (consistency; repentance)

_____

_____

_____

8. Laws against _____ have been challenged in court on the grounds that they violate one's constitutional rights. (proficiency; vagrancy)

_____

_____

_____

9. The principal warned several students that their continued _____ would result in their suspension. (extravagance; truancy)

_____

_____

_____

10. Max was not the greatest second baseman, but his _____ as a batter made him a reliable asset to his team. (consistency; vagrancy)

_____

_____

_____

Test-Taking Strategies

A synonym test asks you to choose a word with the same or nearly the same meaning as another word. For example, *immense* is a synonym for *huge*, and both words are synonyms for *large*. In an attempt to confuse you, test makers sometimes include words with sounds or spellings similar to those of the correct word. The answers may also include an antonym, a word with the opposite meaning of the tested word.

Practice: Choose the <u>synonym</u> for the italicized word in each sentence. Write your choice on the answer line.

1. There were reports of *bogus* 10-dollar bills being passed in town.   1. _____
   (A) genuine   (B) unusual   (C) foreign   (D) fake

2. Before orchids can grow properly, they must have a *conducive*   2. _____
   environment.
   (A) familiar   (B) hostile   (C) favorable   (D) brightly lit

Name _____

How well do you remember the words you studied in Lessons 16 through 18? Take the following test covering the words from the last three lessons.

Part 1 Choose the Correct Meaning

Each question below includes a word in capital letters, followed by four words or phrases. Choose the word or phrase that is <u>closest</u> in meaning to the word in capital letters. Write the letter for your answer on the line provided.

Sample

| S. FINISH | (A) enjoy | (B) complete | S. _____ |
| | (C) destroy | (D) enlarge | |

| 1. PREY | (A) praise | (B) condemn | 1. _____ |
| | (C) victim | (D) official | |

| 2. PUN | (A) bread roll | (B) play on words | 2. _____ |
| | (C) type of poem | (D) opinion | |

| 3. TRUANCY | (A) absence | (B) truthfulness | 3. _____ |
| | (C) homelessness | (D) musical ability | |

| 4. ANTHOLOGY | (A) type of comparison | (B) collection of literary works | 4. _____ |
| | (C) study of prehistoric animals | (D) opposite | |

| 5. SERRATED | (A) burnt | (B) saw-toothed | 5. _____ |
| | (C) dull | (D) enlarged | |

| 6. PROFICIENCY | (A) wealth | (B) love of sports | 6. _____ |
| | (C) ease of motion | (D) skill | |

| 7. FORESHADOW | (A) predict | (B) cover | 7. _____ |
| | (C) outline | (D) delay | |

| 8. EXHUME | (A) extinguish | (B) amuse | 8. _____ |
| | (C) unearth | (D) bury | |

| 9. EXTRAVAGANCE | (A) necessity | (B) pleasurable experience | 9. _____ |
| | (C) type of plant life | (D) luxury | |

| 10. SONNET | (A) type of play | (B) short poem | 10. _____ |
| | (C) wandering musician | (D) article of clothing | |

11. ATTRIBUTE   (A) characteristic   (B) argument   11. _____
                      (C) height   (D) similarity

12. EPIGRAM   (A) secret message   (B) story of a superhero   12. _____
                      (C) witty remark   (D) outer covering

13. RESISTANCE   (A) type of poison   (B) plant growth   13. _____
                      (C) opposition   (D) invitation

14. URGENCY   (A) strong desire   (B) important skill   14. _____
                      (C) group of educated   (D) emergency
                          people

15. REPENTANCE   (A) repeated material   (B) regret   15. _____
                       (C) enemy   (D) enclosure

Part 2 Matching Words and Meaning

Match the definition in Column B with the word in Column A. Write
the letter of the correct definition on the answer line.

Column A	Column B	
16. tragedy	a. overthrow	16. _____
17. stanza	b. nonprofessional	17. _____
18. estimate	c. animal story	18. _____
19. fable	d. play that ends in death	19. _____
20. epic	e. guess	20. _____
21. convenience	f. author's use of one thing to stand for another	21. _____
22. vegetation	g. poem part	22. _____
23. unseat	h. handiness	23. _____
24. symbolism	i. plants	24. _____
25. amateur	j. story of a hero's great deeds	25. _____

Name _____

Coyote Enters the Upper World
–a Nez Percé Story

It is said that, long ago, Native Americans could **assume** the shapes
of animals. The Coyote was their favorite shape because he was the
shrewdest of all the animals. He was not as big as a Grizzly Bear.
In fact, his **meager** body looked more like that of a small dog. He
5 was, however, a master of magic and a clever trickster.

    One day, Coyote overheard a **conclave** of the animals. They
were engaged in an argument over who was the most powerful.
When the arguments grew fierce and the behavior downright
barbarous, Coyote entered the secret meeting and **proposed**
10 a test. Whoever was brave enough to climb the tallest pine to
the Eagle's nest would be named most powerful.

    One by one, the animals tried. Red Squirrel, always in a fog,
forgot what he was doing halfway up and **scurried** down in a
flash. Grizzly Bear's great weight almost snapped the trunk of the
15 tree, forcing him back down. Little Black Bear might have been
successful, but Coyote used magic to make the tree top and nest
rise higher and higher.

    When it was Coyote's turn, he took on his human shape and
warned the other animals not to watch him climb, as it would cause
20 him to lose his powers. At first, Coyote climbed rapidly, but soon he
weakened. "Look away!" Coyote shouted when he saw the animals
looking up at him. They obeyed, and Coyote resumed his **ascent**.
Once again however, his powers began to **deteriorate**. Oh, how he
wished he had not made the tree taller! Coyote kept climbing until
25 he passed through a cloud and into the Upper World. There he met
two spiders whom he recognized as his grandfathers.

    Coyote returned to his animal form so that his grandfathers
would know him. Then he explained what had happened and why
he was too weak to return to earth on his own. The grandfathers
30 handed Coyote a silver thread to lower himself through the clouds
and down to earth. Coyote was not eager to **descend** to earth,
but he held tight and slowly returned to earth.

    On the ground, the other animals were sure Coyote was dead.
When Coyote saw his **bereaved** friends, he told them that the time
35 of the humans was nearing. From that time on, no one would be
allowed to return from the Upper World. The animals listened
attentively, for Coyote proved to be the most powerful of all.

Words
ascent
assume
barbarous
bereaved
conclave
descend
deteriorate
meager
propose
scurry

Unlocking Meaning

Each word in this lesson's word list appears in dark type in the selection you just read. Think about how the vocabulary word is used in the selection. Then write the letter for the best answer to each question.

1. Which word or words could best replace *assume* in line 1?   1. _____
   (A) avoid   (B) take on
   (C) guess   (D) redo

2. Another word for *meager* (line 4) is _____.   2. _____
   (A) scanty   (B) tall
   (C) overweight   (D) awkward

3. A *conclave* (line 6) can be described as a(n) _____.   3. _____
   (A) flat piece of ground   (B) religious community
   (C) agreement   (D) secret gathering

4. Another word for b*arbarous* (line 9) is _____.   4. _____
   (A) savage   (B) civilized
   (C) hairy   (D) private

5. If a test is *proposed* (line 9), it is _____.   5. _____
   (A) examined in detail   (B) discarded without discussion
   (C) changed slightly   (D) suggested for consideration

6. Another word for *scurried* (line 13) is _____.   6. _____
   (A) washed   (B) limped
   (C) dashed   (D) scratched

7. An *ascent* (line 22) is a(n) _____.   7. _____
   (A) unpleasant odor   (B) movement upward
   (C) downward slope   (D) manner of speaking

8. To *deteriorate* (line 23) is to _____.   8. _____
   (A) lessen   (B) recover
   (C) shine   (D) increase

9. To *descend* (line 31) is to _____.   9. _____
   (A) touch   (B) improve
   (C) go down   (D) look carefully

10. If you are *bereaved* (line 34), you have _____.   10. _____
    (A) lost your way   (B) received good news
    (C) fallen asleep   (D) suffered the loss of a loved one

Applying Meaning

Decide which word in parentheses best completes the sentence. Then write the sentence, adding the missing word.

1. The prisoners were given a _____ meal of rice and dried fish. (bereaved; meager)

_____

_____

_____

2. When I turned on the lights, I saw a mouse _____ for its hole. (propose; scurry)

_____

_____

_____

3. The _____ friends of the accident victim left flowers at the scene of the crash. (barbarous; bereaved)

_____

_____

_____

4. The United Nations accused the rebels of committing _____ acts against the civilian population. (barbarous; bereaved)

_____

_____

_____

5. I _____ that we limit the cost of holiday gifts to no more than ten dollars. (propose; scurry)

_____

_____

_____

Read each sentence below. Write "correct" on the answer line if the vocabulary word has been used correctly or "incorrect" if it has been used incorrectly.

6. The *ascent* of the mountain proved to be more difficult than we had expected.

6. _____

7. I had never seen a human being *assume* that much food at one meal.

8. We lifted our eyes to watch the young actress as she gracefully *descended* the staircase leading to the stage.

9. The bear will hibernate in a *conclave* for the winter.

10. Tulips and daffodils swayed gently in a soft breeze; spring *deteriorated* early this year.

7. _____

8. _____

9. _____

10. _____

For each word used incorrectly, write a sentence using the word properly.

_____

_____

_____

_____

_____

_____

_____

_____

Mastering Meaning

According to the Nez Percé tradition, the Great Spirit allowed all things in nature to change into human form as a test for the coming of human beings. If you had the chance, what animal form would you like to change into? What physical attributes and abilities of that animal appeal to you? Write two paragraphs explaining what animal form you would choose and why. Use some of the words you studied in this lesson.

Vocabulary of Thinking and Learning

Name _____

Have you ever heard the expression "Knowledge is power"? Francis Bacon, an English philosopher and essayist, wrote this phrase in 1597. Bacon was obviously aware that knowledge gives people control over their lives. In this lesson, you will learn 10 words associated with thinking and learning.

Unlocking Meaning

Read the sentences or short passages below. Write the letter for the correct definition of the italicized vocabulary word.

1. To attend the *conservatory*, you must pass a tryout and convince a committee that you are dedicated to your art.
   (A) recycling center   (B) music or drama school
   (C) gymnasium   (D) nursing academy

2. I needed time to *contemplate* the job offer for a few days before making a decision.
   (A) request   (B) badger relentlessly
   (C) duplicate exactly   (D) think about carefully

3. Due to a lack of money, the middle school will not be able to offer art as part of its *curriculum*.
   (A) course of study   (B) competition
   (C) weather   (D) meeting area

4. Dr. Van's *intuition* told her the fossils were fakes even before they were examined scientifically.
   (A) a sensing or understanding not based on facts   (B) payment or fees required to attend a school
   (C) close friend   (D) fear or apprehension

5. This is an important decision; you should *mull* over all options before enrolling in advanced chemistry.
   (A) disregard completely   (B) heat slowly
   (C) disassemble   (D) ponder at length

Words

conservatory

contemplate

curriculum

intuition

mull

sage

scholarship

scholastic

seminar

seminary

1. _____

2. _____

3. _____

4. _____

5. _____

6. The king was only a boy, so he had to depend on the *sage* advice
   of his ministers.

   6. _____

   (A) incompetent   (B) wise
   (C) talkative   (D) young

7. His award-winning book on cell structure strengthened Dr. Wong's
   reputation for *scholarship* in the field.

   7. _____

   (A) lack of interest   (B) imitation
   (C) expert knowledge gained   (D) suspicion or distrust
       by study

8. He will have no trouble getting into the college of his choice
   because of his high *scholastic* standing.

   8. _____

   (A) relating to schools or   (B) athletic
       education
   (C) flexible   (D) excited or agitated

9. In their weekly *seminar* the students share their research with each
   other and their instructor.

   9. _____

   (A) massive political protest   (B) library dedicated to one field
       march   of study
   (C) small group of students   (D) wilderness expedition
       studying under a professor

10. After completing her course of studies at the *seminary*, my aunt
    will be an ordained minister.

    10. _____

    (A) prison   (B) field or prairie
    (C) graveyard   (D) school for training clergy

Applying Meaning

Follow the directions below to write a sentence using a vocabulary word.

1. Write a sentence about a police detective. Use the word *intuition* in your sentence.

   _____

   _____

   _____

2. Write a sentence about a school committee meeting. Use the word *curriculum* .

   _____

   _____

   _____

3. Describe someone whose advice you respect. Use the word *sage* in your sentence.

   _____

   _____

   _____

4. Describe someone with a musical talent. Use the word *conservatory*.

   _____

   _____

   _____

5. Write a sentence about a work of art. Use a form of the word *contemplate* in your sentence.

   _____

   _____

   _____

Each question below contains a vocabulary word from this lesson. Answer each question "yes" or "no" in the space provided

6. Might an angry bear *mull* a smaller animal?   6. _____

7. Would *scholastic* ability help you achieve good grades in school?   7. _____

8. Does one often encounter grieving relatives at a *seminar*?   8. _____

9. Might a student read textbooks to improve his *scholarship* in a specific field of study?

9. _____

10. Would someone needing surgery go directly to a *seminary*?

10. _____

For each question you answered "no," write a sentence explaining your reason.

_____

_____

_____

_____

_____

_____

_____

_____

Cultural Literacy Note

Proverbs

Proverbs are sayings that offer bits of wisdom or advice. Everyone has heard "An apple a day keeps the doctor away." Some proverbs seem to conflict with one another. You may have heard the expression "You can't teach an old dog new tricks." Compare this to the proverb "You're never too old to learn." These seem to be directly opposite. However, each may be correct in different circumstances.

Cooperative Learning: With a partner, discuss these seemingly contradictory proverbs: "Knowledge is power," "Ignorance is bliss"; "Look before you leap," "He who hesitates is lost." For each pair of proverbs, decide whether both of them can be true.

Name _____

The Latin word *cedere* means "to go" or "to yield." This Latin word appears in English words as *-cede-* or *-cess-*. The Latin word *mittere* means "to send." Elements of this word appear in English words as the roots *-mit-* or *-mis-*. Knowing these roots will help you unlock the meaning of many English words.

Root	Meaning	English Word
-cede-	to go, to yield	intercede
-cess-		predecessor
-mit-	to send	omit
-mis-		permissible

Unlocking Meaning

A vocabulary word appears in italics in each sentence or short passage below. Find the root in the vocabulary word and think about how the word is used in the passage. Then write a definition for the vocabulary word. Compare your definition with the definition in the dictionary at the back of the book.

1. Because of the danger, only the work crew had *access* to the blasting area.

   _____
   _____
   _____

2. Doing research for my family tree, I was surprised to learn that an *ancestor* of mine worked with Abraham Lincoln.

   _____
   _____
   _____

3. The names of my *deceased* aunt and other victims of the tornado are listed on a plaque in our church.

   _____
   _____
   _____

Words

access

ancestor

deceased

exceed

intercede

omit

permissible

predecessor

remittance

submit

4. The weather report said the temperature could *exceed* ninety degrees, a record for this date.

_____

_____

_____

5. When my brother and I quarrel, my mother tries not to *intercede*. She wants us to settle things on our own.

_____

_____

_____

6. Copy every word of the quotation carefully. If you *omit* just one word, you may change the author's meaning.

_____

_____

_____

7. Even though it is *permissible* for seniors to leave school after their last class, many stay for after-school activities.

_____

_____

_____

8. Since they seemed to work well, Mayor Marlow continued many of the programs introduced by her *predecessor*.

_____

_____

_____

9. Please enclose the dated coupon with your *remittance* when making your monthly car payment.

_____

_____

_____

10. The editor asked reporters to *submit* their articles no later than Tuesday so he would have time to review them.

_____

_____

_____

Applying Meaning

Write the vocabulary word or a form of the vocabulary word that fits each clue below. Then use the word in a sentence.

1. Your great-great-grandparents are examples of these.

_____

_____

_____

2. A key will provide this to the contents of the treasure chest.

_____

_____

_____

3. A lawyer may do this with the judge on behalf of someone he represents.

_____

_____

_____

4. George Washington, Abraham Lincoln, and George Bush were three of President Clinton's.

_____

_____

_____

5. After you fill out an entry blank, you must do this with it if you want to win the contest.

_____

_____

_____

6. It is the opposite of alive.

_____

_____

_____

7. If a driver does this to the speed limit, he may get a ticket.

_____

_____

_____

Write each sentence. Add the correct form of the word in parentheses.

8. We had to _____ twenty-five dollars to the soccer association by May 1 to be in the tournament. (remittance)

_____

_____

_____

9. Every student knows that only teachers are _____ in the faculty lounge. (permissible)

_____

_____

_____

10. When I realized that I'd forgotten to put Joy's name on the list, I apologized for the _____. (omit)

_____

_____

_____

Using the Dictionary

A dictionary may give several meanings for one word. Each meaning is numbered. Sometimes sample phrases or sentences are provided to make the meanings clear. Look at the sample entry below.

com•pose (kəm pōz') *v.* **com•posed, com•pos•ing, com•pos•es. 1.** To create or put together: *compose a symphony.* **2.** To make calm: *compose oneself before a test.*

Look up the following words in a dictionary. Use each word in two sentences, using a different meaning in each sentence.

recess   admission   mark   face

Name _____

How well do you remember the words you studied in Lessons 19 through 21? Take the following test covering the words from the last three lessons.

Part 1 Choose the Correct Meaning

Each question below includes a word in capital letters, followed by four words or phrases. Choose the word or phrase that is closest in meaning to the word in capital letters. Write the letter for your answer on the line provided.

Sample

| S. FINISH | (A) enjoy | (B) complete | S. _____ |
| | (C) destroy | (D) enlarge | |

| 1. DECEASED | (A) reduced | (B) stopped | 1. _____ |
| | (C) dead | (D) counted | |

| 2. PROPOSE | (A) situate | (B) arrange | 2. _____ |
| | (C) suggest | (D) create | |

| 3. OMIT | (A) allow | (B) force | 3. _____ |
| | (C) stress | (D) leave out | |

| 4. CONCLAVE | (A) indented | (B) secret meeting | 4. _____ |
| | (C) hollow | (D) class | |

| 5. MULL | (A) reject | (B) read | 5. _____ |
| | (C) discuss | (D) think | |

| 6. CONTEMPLATE | (A) consider | (B) pattern | 6. _____ |
| | (C) arrange for | (D) select | |

| 7. REMITTANCE | (A) contract | (B) signature | 7. _____ |
| | (C) mistake | (D) payment | |

| 8. SCURRY | (A) infect | (B) scamper | 8. _____ |
| | (C) jump | (D) stroll | |

| 9. INTERCEDE | (A) overhear | (B) recommend | 9. _____ |
| | (C) step in | (D) neglect | |

| 10. SAGE | (A) wise | (B) lucky | 10. _____ |
| | (C) polite | (D) weak | |

| 11. MEAGER | (A) excited | (B) short | 11. _____ |
| | (C) hairy | (D) slight | |

12. EXCEED (A) remain at (B) equal 12. _____
(C) fall short of (D) surpass

13. ANCESTOR (A) grandchild (B) forefather 13. _____
(C) relative (D) friend

14. CONSERVATORY (A) business school (B) music or drama school 14. _____

(C) type of laboratory (D) elected representatives

15. BARBAROUS (A) brutal (B) friendly 15. _____
(C) unpredictable (D) amusing

Part 2 Matching Words and Meanings

Match the definition in Column B with the word in Column A. Write the letter of the correct definition on the line provided.

Column A	Column B	
16. bereaved	a. upward movement	16. _____
17. permissible	b. having suffered a loss	17. _____
18. scholastic	c. to lose quality or amount	18. _____
19. access	d. course of study	19. _____
20. ascent	e. instinctive knowledge	20. _____
21. predecessor	f. related to school	21. _____
22. curriculum	g. school for training priests, ministers, or rabbis	22. _____
23. deteriorate	h. right to enter or use	23. _____
24. intuition	i. allowed	24. _____
25. seminary	j. one who comes before	25 _____

Name _____

Matthew Henson, Arctic Explorer

Matthew Henson was born in 1866 on a Maryland farm. As an African American, Henson had few **options** for earning a livelihood. Therefore, when he was 13 years old, he decided to run away and hire himself out as a cabin boy on a vessel bound for France and
5 the Philippines. The ship's captain liked Henson and urged him to **utilize** the ship's library to learn **navigation**. Henson studied hard and applied what he learned as the ship traveled from one exotic **locale** to another.

After the captain died, Henson tried to make a life for himself
10 on land, but racial **prejudice** discouraged African Americans from seeking **lofty** positions, so Henson took whatever lowly work he was offered. This included a job as a stock boy in a naval supply store. That job, however, was a turning point, for it was there that Henson met Robert E. Peary, a civil engineer for the United States
15 Navy. Henson was **intrigued** by Peary and asked to accompany him on his next voyage.

Over the next 20 years, Peary made seven trips to the Arctic. Henson became an invaluable member of Peary's crew, acting mainly as Peary's personal attendant. Henson also learned the Inuit language
20 and helped establish a solid working relationship between the native people of the Arctic region and Peary's crew.

It was on the 1908-1909 voyage that Peary decided to locate the North Pole. The journey was **arduous**. Peary sent back all the members of his party except for Henson and four Inuit guides. Henson's
25 ability to communicate with the guides in their own language and his knowledge of navigation made him **indispensable**. Suffering from exhaustion and frostbite, Peary left Henson the task of discovering the Pole. On April 6,1909, the former cabin boy became the first person to stand on the North Pole. Peary could barely lift his
30 arm as Henson placed an American flag on the northernmost spot on Earth.

Upon their return, Peary and his crew were honored with medals and **adulation**. Henson did not receive any glory until more than 30 years later. In 1944, 11 years before he died, Henson
35 was finally awarded the Congressional Medal of Honor.

Words

adulation

arduous

indispensable

intrigue

locale

lofty

navigation

option

prejudice

utilize

Each word in this lesson's word list appears in dark type in the selection you just read. Think about how the vocabulary word is used in the selection, then write the letter for the best answer to each question.

1. Another word for *options* in line 2 is _____.
   (A) choices   (B) houses
   (C) boats   (D) sayings

   1. _____

2. Which word or words could best replace *utilize* in line 6?
   (A) clean out   (B) live in
   (C) destroy   (D) make use of

   2. _____

3. *Navigation* (line 6) has to do with _____.
   (A) growing vegetables at sea   (B) directing the course of a ship
   (C) shipbuilding   (D) farming techniques

   3. _____

4. A *locale* (line 8) is a(n) _____.
   (A) injection   (B) insane person
   (C) place   (D) friend or neighbor

   4. _____

5. Another word for *prejudice* (line 10) is _____.
   (A) bigotry   (B) fear
   (C) disease   (D) loneliness

   5. _____

6. Which word could best replace *lofty* in line 11?
   (A) insignificant   (B) important
   (C) heavenly   (D) heavy

   6. _____

7. If someone *intrigued* (line 15) you, they _____.
   (A) captured your interest   (B) ignored you and your ideas
   (C) interviewed you   (D) disliked you

   7. _____

8. An *arduous* (line 23) journey is one that is _____.
   (A) unexpected   (B) swift and effortless
   (C) uneventful but satisfying (D) extremely long and difficult

   8. _____

9. Another word for *indispensable* (line 26) is _____.
   (A) unimportant   (B) replaceable
   (C) essential   (D) awkward

   9. _____

10. *Adulation* (line 33) means _____.
    (A) disapproval and blame   (B) the process of maturing
    (C) the act of rising and falling (D) great praise and recognition

    10. _____

Applying Meaning

Each question below contains a vocabulary word from this lesson. Answer each question "yes" or "no" in the space provided.

1. Would a person who commits a vicious crime expect to receive public *adulation*?

2. Is it more *arduous* to climb a mountain in winter than it is in summer?

3. Should an *indispensable* employee worry about losing her job?

4. Could a shipwreck be the result of poor *navigation*?

5. Are King and Queen *lofty* titles?

6. Do people with a variety of *prejudices* make good jurors?

1. _____

2. _____

3. _____

4. _____

5. _____

6. _____

For each question you answered "no," write a sentence explaining your reason.

_____

_____

_____

_____

_____

_____

_____

_____

_____

_____

_____

_____

Decide which word in parentheses best completes the sentence. Then write the sentence, adding the missing word.

7. After graduation, Ed had two _____; he could work for his dad or go to college. (locales; options)

_____

_____

_____

8. She is a skilled pianist who plans to _____ her talents in the school orchestra. (intrigue; utilize)

_____

_____

_____

9. The idea of traveling to Mars has always _____ me. (intrigued; utilized)

_____

_____

_____

10. Each week, the show comes from a different _____; last week, it was broadcast from New Orleans. (locale; option)

_____

_____

_____

Mastering Meaning

Look up some facts about the discovery of the North Pole. Why was it important? What hardships were faced? How many people were in the original expedition? Write a report on your findings. Use some of the words you studied in this lesson.

Vocabulary of Travel and Movement

Name _____

People move about in many ways and for many reasons. There are numerous words in our language for how we walk and the types of moves we make. Other words stand for the trips we like to take or, in some cases, cause others to take. In this lesson you will learn 10 words associated with our many ways of coming and going.

Unlocking Meaning

Read the sentences or short passages below. Write the letter for the correct definition of the italicized vocabulary word.

1. On Sundays, my sister and I go to the shore. We never rush; we just *amble* along and talk.
   (A) hop up and down   (B) walk at an easy, slow pace
   (C) move quickly   (D) turn around in circles

2. Because we kept getting in his way, Dad had to *banish* us from the kitchen while he prepared dinner.
   (A) invite in   (B) show or display
   (C) wave excitedly   (D) force to leave

3. The game was so one-sided and boring that the crowd could not *bestir* itself to cheer when the home team finally scored.
   (A) provoke to action   (B) defeat
   (C) accidentally overlook   (D) confuse

4. The newborn horse stood on wobbly legs and moved toward its mother with an unsteady *gait*.
   (A) manner of speaking   (B) aggravation
   (C) way of walking   (D) expression

5. Since my aunt retired, she likes to take vacations. Last week she made a quick *jaunt* to Bermuda.
   (A) short, pleasant journey (B) large package
   (C) imprisonment   (D) brief, uplifting speech

6. The manager does not want students with nothing to do after school to *loiter* in the mall.
   (A) yell loudly   (B) stand around aimlessly
   (C) roll over   (D) rush by without stopping

Words

amble
banish
bestir
gait
jaunt
loiter
promenade
saunter
sojourn
tarry

1. _____

2. _____

3. _____

4. _____

5. _____

6. _____

7. On Founder's Day, the townspeople dress in old-fashioned clothes
and *promenade* through the park as they did years ago.
    (A) squeeze tightly   (B) whistle like a bird
    (C) lift or raise   (D) go on a leisurely stroll

7. _____

8. When I saw my brother *saunter* into the house with a superior
look on his face, I knew he had gotten an A on the test.
    (A) fall down   (B) stroll happily at an unhurried
                          pace
    (C) spin wildly   (D) heat to a high temperature

8. _____

9. While we're vacationing on Cape Cod, we'll *sojourn* at Martha's
Vineyard for a few days.
    (A) wail in anguish   (B) lie blatantly
    (C) stay for a short time   (D) surrender without any
                              conditions

9. _____

10. We are supposed to leave the city on Friday, but we may *tarry* an
extra day to attend the theater on Saturday.
    (A) delay   (B) examine closely
    (C) protest loudly   (D) move in a unpredictable
                              manner

10. _____

Applying Meaning

Follow the directions below to write a sentence using a vocabulary word.

1. Describe a day when you had nothing to do. Use any form of the word *loiter*.

   _____

   _____

   _____

2. Use any form of the word *saunter* to describe a day with a friend.

   _____

   _____

   _____

3. Use the word *jaunt* in a sentence about a trip you have taken.

   _____

   _____

   _____

4. Write a sentence about a fictional kingdom. Use any form of the word *banish* in your sentence.

   _____

   _____

   _____

5. Describe someone hearing the alarm clock buzz on Monday morning. Use any form of the word *bestir*.

   _____

   _____

   _____

Decide which word in parentheses best completes the sentence. Then write the sentence, adding the missing word.

6. Lydia's distinctive _____ is both a walk and a skip. {gait; jaunt)

   _____

   _____

   _____

7. I missed the school bus and had to walk home. I should not have _____ with my friends after school. (bestirred; tarried)

_____

_____

_____

8. Martin was in no particular hurry, so he _____ home from the store. (ambled; sojourned)

_____

_____

_____

9. Presidents of the United States often _____ at Camp David to relax from the pressures of the office. (sojourn; amble)

_____

_____

_____

10. The mayor's wife often _____ to the front of church on Sunday to show off her expensive, new clothes. (promenades; tarries)

_____

_____

_____

Our Living Language

gait

In addition to meaning a particular way of moving on foot, the word *gait* also refers to the several ways that a horse can walk or run. Depending on the rhythm and order in which a horse lifts its feet, its gait is called a *canter* or a *trot*.

Do Some Research: Use a reference book such as an encyclopedia to determine the difference between a canter and a trot. Report your findings to the class.

The Roots -vert- and -verse-

Lesson
24
Part A

Name _____

The Latin word *vertere* means "to turn." It appears in English words as the root *-vert-* or *-verse-*. You see it in words such as *reverse* and *revert*. In this lesson, you will learn 10 words with the *-vert-* and *-verse-* roots.

Root	Meaning	English Word
-vert-	to turn	extrovert
-verse-		reversible

Unlocking Meaning

A vocabulary word appears in italics in each sentence or short passage below. Find the root in the vocabulary word and think about how the word is used in the passage. Then write a definition for the vocabulary word. Compare your definition with the definition in the dictionary at the back of the book.

1. The city wants to *convert* the vacant lot into a park so the neighborhood children will have a safe place to play.

   _____

   _____

   _____

2. The fight was just a *diversion*. While people watched the brawl, the movie star entered the hotel unnoticed by his fans.

   _____

   _____

   _____

3. The exhibit displayed the *diversity* of plant life in this area. Over 100 different species were included.

   _____

   _____

   _____

4. Jill is quiet and thoughtful. Her brother is an *extrovert* who would rather talk than listen.

   _____

   _____

   _____

Words

convert

diversion

diversity

extrovert

introvert

invert

reversible

revert

version

versus

Copyright © Glencoe/McGraw-Hill, a division of The McGraw-Hill Companies, Inc.

5. Sid is an *introvert*. He would rather spend the afternoon in his room reading than doing things with friends.

_____

_____

_____

6. Place a dish over the top of the pan; then carefully *invert* the pan. The omelet should plop onto the dish.

_____

_____

_____

7. One side of Maya's *reversible* jacket is dark blue; the other side is red-and-blue plaid.

_____

_____

_____

8. England leased Hong Kong from China in 1898, with the understanding that control of the island would eventually *revert* to China.

_____

_____

_____

9. In the original *version* of the story the hero dies, but in the movie he returns home safely.

_____

_____

_____

10. When it comes to hurricanes and tornadoes, it is mankind *versus* Mother Nature. Mother Nature usually wins.

_____

_____

_____

Applying Meaning

Read each sentence below. Write "correct" on the answer line if the vocabulary word has been used correctly or "incorrect" if it has been used incorrectly.

1. Eventually the tadpole will *invert* into a frog.

2. I wouldn't describe myself as an *introvert*. I get quite bored and restless when I'm left to myself for very long.

3. We sang the first two *versus* of the song in English and the third in French.

4. I've seen both *versions* of the movie, but I can't decide whether I prefer the old one or the new one.

5. Carla is such an *extrovert* that she refuses to attend dances or join in after-school activities.

6. She knew how many rows and seats were in the theater and used *diversion* to figure out the number of seats in each row.

1. _____

2. _____

3. _____

4. _____

5. _____

6. _____

For each word used incorrectly, write a sentence using the word properly.

_____

_____

_____

_____

_____

_____

_____

_____

_____

_____

Write each sentence below, adding a form of the word in parentheses.

7. The Supreme Court _____ the decision of the lower court.
(reversible)

_____

_____

_____

8. After the back taxes were paid, ownership of the apartment _____ to the former landlord. (revert)

_____

_____

_____

9. They came from _____ backgrounds, but they were all united in their belief that violence must end. (diversity)

_____

_____

_____

10. _____ the military base into an airport will take several years. (convert)

_____

_____

_____

Test-Taking Strategies

Some tests include antonym questions, which ask you to choose the word that means the opposite of a given word. These tests may try to trick you by including a synonym for the word as one of the answers. Remember that the test asks for the word that means the <u>opposite</u> of the first word. Also, remember that words can have several meanings. Be sure to consider all meanings of a word.

Practice: Write the letter for the word that is most nearly opposite in meaning to the given word.

1. SPORADIC   (A) disheveled   (B) continuous   1. _____
              (C) wasteful   (D) occasional   (E) irritable

2. IMPUDENT   (A) rude   (B) cautious   2. _____
              (C) unwise   (D) stationary   (E) courteous

3. REPUGNANT   (A) cowardly   (B) disagreeable   3. _____
              (C) appealing   (D) boring   (E) simple

4. FRIVOLOUS   (A) serious   (B) poor   4. _____
              (C) lengthy   (D) foolish   (E) stainless

5. PACIFY   (A) expose   (B) arouse   5. _____
              (C) separate   (D) comfort   (E) deny

Name _____

How well do you remember the words you studied in Lessons 22 through 24? Take the following test covering the words from the last three lessons.

Part 1 Antonyms

Each question below includes a word in capital letters, followed by four words or phrases. Choose the word or phrase that is most nearly <u>opposite</u> in meaning to the words in capital letters. Write the letter for your answer on the line provided.

Sample

S. SLOW	(A) lazy (C) fast	(B) simple (D) common	S. _____
1. DIVERSITY	(A) similarity (C) originality	(B) longevity (D) texture	1. _____
2. BANISH	(A) greet (C) hide	(B) prevent (D) welcome	2. _____
3. LOFTY	(A) significant (C) responsible	(B) unrestricted (D) lowly	3. _____
4. INTROVERT	(A) intelligent (C) creative	(B) outgoing (D) forgetful	4. _____
5. ARDUOUS	(A) long (C) easy	(B) frequent (D) repetitive	5. _____
6. INDISPENSABLE	(A) broken (C) new	(B) unnecessary (D) colorful	6. _____
7. VERSUS	(A) in favor of (C) without	(B) plus (D) before	7. _____
8. LOITER	(A) hurry (C) shop	(B) rest (D) notice	8. _____
9. PREJUDICE	(A) misunderstanding (C) fairness	(B) attitude (D) habit	9. _____
10. REVERSIBLE	(A) unlimited (C) untouched	(B) unchangeable (D) unfolded	10. _____
11. INTRIGUE	(A) confuse (C) frighten	(B) overwhelm (D) bore	11. _____

12. REVERT (A) release   (B) conceal   12. _____
       (C) go forward (D) reconsider

13. AMBLE   (A) dance   (B) drive   13. _____
       (C) rush   (D) march

14. BESTIR   (A) deaden   (B) arouse   14. _____
       (C) convince   (D) unite

15. ADULATION (A) commentary (B) questions 15. _____
       (C) explanation (D) criticism

Part 2 Matching Words and Meanings

Match the definition in Column B with the word in Column A. Write the letter of the correct definition on the line provided.

Column A   **Column B**

16. diversion   a. place   16. _____

17. utilize   b. choice   17. _____

18. saunter   c. use   18. _____

19. locale   d. change   19. _____

20. invert   e. a short trip   20. _____

21. jaunt   f. walk leisurely 21. _____

22. option   g. stay   22. _____

23. tarry   h. distraction   23. _____

24. version   i. turn upside down 24. _____

25. convert   j. account   25. _____

World Habitats

The earth is divided into separate ecological systems, or biomes, as they are sometimes called. The divisions are based upon climate and vegetation. Within each system are ecological communities that sustain their own plant and animal habitats.

5   The seemingly barren region that **encircles** the North Pole is marked by long, cold winters. Nevertheless, it is home to many types of plants and animals. Mosses and grasses exist in the frozen tundra. Bears, moose, ducks, weasels, and squirrels can also be found there.

10   **Frigid**, dry, and icy, Antarctica at the South Pole is almost **devoid** of plants. Surprisingly, though, it is rich in animal life, which **thrives**, thanks to **nourishment** provided by the sea. Microscopic sea life feeds multitudes of tiny floating animals called zooplankton. These become food for a variety of birds, fish, and mammals.

15   Even more **uninhabitable** than the regions at the polar tips of the earth is the desert. Extreme heat and a lack of water make this a hostile environment for living organisms. Nevertheless, many plants, such as cacti, and animals, such as camels, lizards, and other reptiles, have managed to survive in these hot, dry conditions.

20   Not as dry as deserts nor as moist as forests or jungles, grasslands are most abundant in the **temperate** regions of the earth. Grasslands boast a wide **array** of wildlife. Plants, insects, reptiles, birds, and a wide assortment of mammals can be found in the grasslands. Savannas are tropical grasslands with trees, shrubs, and grasses that 25 support exotic wildlife. The African savanna, for example, is home to herds of wildebeest, elephants, and gazelles, as well as black rhinoceros, giraffes, hippopotamuses, and lions.

    Jungles support the greatest variety of plant and animal life on earth. Although they cover less than 6 percent of the world's land 30 surface, these regions are the habitats for **innumerable** species of plants and animals. Their rainy, hot climate is ideal for supporting dense plant growth and large numbers of animals.

    Because climate changes with altitude, a mountain can contain more than one ecological system. Mountains are the home of 35 predators, such as snow leopards and golden eagles. These animals can **coexist** in a mountain setting with foragers, such as Himalayan ibexes and Alpine voles.

Words
array
coexist
devoid
encircle
frigid
innumerable
nourishment
temperate
thrive
uninhabitable

Each word in this lesson's word list appears in dark type in the selection you just read. Think about how the vocabulary word is used in the selection. Then write the letter for the best answer to each question.

1. Which words could best replace *encircles* in line 5?
   (A) forms a ring around   (B) causes conflict with
   (C) is farthest from   (D) rains heavily on

   1. _____

2. *Frigid* (line 10) means _____.
   (A) furious   (B) stiff or unbending
   (C) extremely cold   (D) hungry

   2. _____

3. If an area is *devoid* (line 10) of plants, it is _____.
   (A) depending on the existence   (B) ideal for the growth of plants
        of plants
   (C) displaying a variety of plant   (D) completely lacking any plants
        species

   3. _____

4. To *thrive* (line 11) is to _____.
   (A) wander aimlessly   (B) grow vigorously
   (C) attack without cause or   (D) disappear suddenly
        reason

   4. _____

5. *Nourishment* (line 12) is a _____.
   (A) clear view   (B) moisture
   (C) substance necessary for   (D) period of unrest
        development

   5. _____

6. If an area is *uninhabitable* (line 15), it is _____.
   (A) unfit to be lived in   (B) different from what is expected
   (C) pleasant and calm   (D) existing beneath the surface

   6. _____

7. *Temperate* (line 21) means _____.
   (A) overcome with   (B) unbearably humid
        blistering heat
   (C) having a mild or moderate   (D) frozen solid
        climate

   7. _____

8. Which word could best replace *array* in line 22?
   (A) territory   (B) display
   (C) view   (D) statement

   8. _____

9. *Innumerable* (line 30) means _____.
   (A) too many to be counted   (B) only one specific type of
   (C) hardly any   (D) filled with sorrow

   9. _____

10. To *coexist* (line 36) is to _____.
    (A) burrow into an under-   (B) practice obvious deceit
         ground tunnel or den
    (C) peacefully attempt to solve   (D) live in the same time or place
         a conflict

    10. _____

Applying Meaning

Decide which word in parentheses best completes the sentence. Then write the sentence, adding the missing word.

1. A well-balanced diet provides more _____ than a diet of sweets and junk food. (frigid; nourishment)

    _____

    _____

    _____

2. My grandfather is always very serious and completely _____ of a sense of humor. (devoid; temperate)

    _____

    _____

    _____

3. Dinosaurs became extinct million of years before humans walked the earth; the two species never _____. (coexisted; encircled)

    _____

    _____

    _____

4. Because I prefer a _____ climate, I would not live in Alaska or Arizona. (devoid; temperate)

    _____

    _____

    _____

5. The trees and shrubs that _____ our yard provide a natural fence around our property. (encircle; nourish)

    _____

    _____

    _____

6. Parts of Alaska have a pleasant summer, but much of the state endures _____ winters. (frigid; innumerable)

    _____

    _____

    _____

7. Lewis and Clark encountered _____ difficulties on their journey.
   (innumerable; nourishing)

   _____

   _____

   _____

Follow the directions below to write a sentence using a vocabulary word.

8. Describe a zoological park. Use the word *array*.

   _____

   _____

   _____

9. Write a sentence about gardening. Use a form of the word *thrive*.

   _____

   _____

   _____

10. Write a sentence about a planet. Use the word *uninhabitable* in
    your sentence.

    _____

    _____

    _____

Mastering Meaning

In addition to the types of ecological systems, or biomes, described
earlier in this lesson, there are also several other types—the steppe,
forest, intertidal, and swamp biomes. Choose one of these biomes and
research its climate, vegetation, and animal population. Write a short
report about the biome you selected. Use some of the words you
have studied in this lesson.

Words from Foreign Languages

Name _____

If the English language doesn't have a word for something, we often just borrow a word from another language. Captain Cook used the Polynesian word *taboo* in his journals. Now it's part of the English language. *Smorgasbord* came from Swedish, and *embargo* from Spanish. In this lesson you will learn 10 English words that have been "borrowed" from other languages.

Unlocking Meaning

A vocabulary word appears in italics in each short passage below. Think about how the word is used. Then write a definition for the vocabulary word. Compare your definition with the one in the dictionary at the back of the book.

1. If we ordered *à la carte,* the salad was an extra $5.99, but it was included in the price of the special.

   _____

   _____

   _____

2. Many of their friends went to the dock to wave good-bye and wish them *bon voyage*.

   _____

   _____

   _____

3. A fake diamond ring was left on the counter as a *decoy* to catch the shoplifter.

   _____

   _____

   _____

4. The *delicatessen* on the corner serves great pastrami sandwiches. The dill pickles and coleslaw are terrific too.

   _____

   _____

   _____

Words
à la carte
bon voyage
decoy
delicatessen
embargo
menagerie
renegade
siesta
smorgasbord
taboo

5. The United States placed an embargo on trade with South Africa in the 1980s.

_____

_____

_____

6. The most unusual animals in the exotic *menagerie* were a leopard with no spots and a giant lizard.

_____

_____

_____

7. Jesse James is one of the West's best-known *renegades*. He robbed banks, stagecoaches, and trains.

_____

_____

_____

8. After a one-hour *siesta*, Leonard awoke refreshed and eager to get back to work.

_____

_____

_____

9. Out hosts offered a *smorgasbord* of meat, vegetables, fruit, salads, and desserts.

_____

_____

_____

10. In some places, it is *taboo* for women to show their faces in public, so females wear veils and head coverings.

_____

_____

_____

Applying Meaning

Write the vocabulary word that fits each clue below. Then use the word in a sentence.

1. It comes from the French *bon voyage*, meaning "good journey."

_____

_____

_____

2. The German word *delikatessen* has the same meaning.

_____

_____

_____

3. It comes from the Spanish *sexta hora*, "sixth hour." Perhaps this was a good time to take a nap.

_____

_____

_____

4. It comes from the Dutch *de kooi*, meaning "the cage."

_____

_____

_____

5. In French it means "by the menu." Be careful; this could get expensive.

_____

_____

_____

Decide which word in parentheses best completes the sentence. Then write the sentence, adding the missing word.

6. In our house, it is strictly _____ to eat snacks in the living room. (à la carte; taboo)

_____

_____

_____

7. Each year we have a neighborhood party with music, dancing, and a(n) _____ of homemade dishes. (embargo; smorgasbord)

_____

_____

_____

8. The circus posters advertised a _____ of exotic animals from Asia and Africa. (menagerie; siesta)

_____

_____

_____

9. Several senators demanded a(n) _____ be placed on sales of computers to the hostile nation. (delicatessen; embargo)

_____

_____

_____

10. In the 1800s, sheriffs in the West spent much of their time pursuing _____ and other outlaws. (decoys; renegades)

_____

_____

_____

Spelling and Meaning

Adding -ed or -ing

When adding *-ed* or *-ing* to a one-syllable word ending in a single vowel and a single consonant, double the final consonant before adding *-ed* or *-ing*. For words with more than one syllable, the final consonant is doubled only if the final syllable is stressed.

jump	jumped	jumping
chop	chopped	chopping
wonder	wondered	wondering
refer	referred	referring

Practice the Strategy: Add *-ed* and *-ing* to each of these words:

commit	enter	expel	grab	travel

Name _____

The prefix *in-* comes from the Latin *in-*, meaning "not." When added to a word or root, it reverses the meaning of the word or root. For example, something that is not active is inactive. When this prefix is added to words beginning with *b*, *m*, or *p*, its spelling changes to *im-*.

Prefix	Meaning	Word
in-	not	incompetent
im-	not	improbable

Unlocking Meaning

A vocabulary word appears in italics in each sentence below. The meaning of the root is given in parentheses. Look at the prefix and think about how the word is used in the passage. Then write a definition for the vocabulary word. Compare your definition with the dictionary definition at the back of the book.

1. These *immature* trees will eventually grow to a height of one hundred feet. (Root word: *maturus*, ripe)

   _____

   _____

   _____

2. The principal heard an *immoderate* amount of noise coming from the unattended classroom. (Root word: *moderatum*, regulated)

   _____

   _____

   _____

3. May's table manners were *impeccable*. (Root word: *peccare*, to sin)

   _____

   _____

   _____

4. The castle walls and wide moat presented an *impenetrable* fortress to the attackers. (Root word: *penitus*, deeply)

   _____

   _____

   _____

Words

immature

immoderate

impeccable

impenetrable

improbable

inaccessible

inaudible

incoherent

incompetent

indecisive

5. The book's *improbable* ending came as a surprise to the disappointed critics. (Root word: *probare*, to prove)

_____

_____

_____

6. The crash site was *inaccessible* by land, so rescuers were brought in by helicopter. (Root word: *accedere*, to arrive)

_____

_____

_____

7. Mel whispered the secret to me so his words would be *inaudible* to others in the room. (Root word: *audire*, to hear)

_____

_____

_____

8. The newspaper article was an *incoherent* jumble of unrelated information. (Root word: *cohaerere*, to cling together)

_____

_____

_____

9. The comedy was about an *incompetent* spy who bungled every assignment he was given. (Root word: *competere*, to be suitable)

_____

_____

_____

10. Because he often delayed important decisions, the mayor appeared to be weak and *indecisive*. (Root word: *decidere*, to decide)

_____

_____

_____

Applying Meaning

Decide which word in parentheses best completes the sentence. Then write the sentence, adding the missing word.

1. The high-pitched sound was _____ to humans, but the barking dogs seemed to hear it. (impenetrable; inaudible)

   _____

   _____

   _____

2. The files in this database are top-secret and _____ without the correct password. (inaccessible; indecisive)

   _____

   _____

   _____

3. The first draft of my report was _____, so I made an outline to organize my ideas. (immoderate; incoherent)

   _____

   _____

   _____

4. The pilot could not see through the _____ clouds and had to rely on radar. (immature; impenetrable)

   _____

   _____

   _____

5. President Truman was rarely _____ when it came to important matters like defending Korea. (indecisive; impeccable)

   _____

   _____

   _____

Each question below contains a vocabulary word from this lesson. Answer each question "yes" or "no" in the space provided.

6. Would a parent be likely to respond favorably to *immoderate* requests from a child?

6. _____

7. Do worms hide from birds so they will be *impeccable*?

7. _____

8. Is it *improbable* for the majority of students in a school to get perfect grades for the entire school year?

8. _____

9. Would you want an *incompetent* surgeon to take out your appendix?

9. _____

10. Might an *immature* teenager whine and throw temper tantrums?

10. _____

For each question you answered "no," write a sentence explaining your reason.

_____

_____

_____

_____

_____

_____

_____

_____

_____

Bonus Word

inexorable

The word *inexorable* means "impossible to persuade with pleas or arguments." It combines three roots in an unusual way. The *in-* prefix means "not," as expected. The prefix *ex-* means "out," or "out of." The root comes from the Latin word *orare*, meaning "to argue or pray." If your teacher makes inexorable demands, you will be unable to pray or argue your way out of them.

Use the Dictionary: Use an unabridged dictionary to look up the definitions and the root meanings of these words: inertia, inexplicable, infallible, impudent, immaculate.

Name _____

How well do you remember the words you studied in Lessons 25 through 27? Take the following test covering the words from the last three lessons.

Part 1 Choose the Correct Meaning

Each question below includes a word in capital letters, followed by four words or phrases. Choose the word or phrase that is <u>closest</u> in meaning to the word in capital letters. Write the letter for your answer on the line provided.

Sample

S. FINISH	(A) enjoy	(B) complete	S. _____
	(C) destroy	(D) enlarge	

1. EMBARGO	(A) agreement	(B) restriction	1. _____
	(C) tax	(D) quota	
2. IMPECCABLE	(A) grotesque	(B) flawless	2. _____
	(C) pitiful	(D) ridiculous	
3. DEVOID	(A) not valid	(B) filled	3. _____
	(C) discouraged	(D) lacking	
4. COEXIST	(A) live together	(B) oppose	4. _____
	(C) direct	(D) avoid	
5. THRIVE	(A) die	(B) explore	5. _____
	(C) prosper	(D) wander	
6. INCOMPETENT	(A) unfit	(B) unusual	6. _____
	(C) untested	(D) unlicensed	
7. NOURISHMENT	(A) light	(B) housing	7. _____
	(C) care	(D) food	
8. SIESTA	(A) afternoon	(B) nap	8. _____
	(C) conversation	(D) walk	
9. IMPROBABLE	(A) unlikely	(B) unpopular	9. _____
	(C) unexplored	(D) uncounted	
10. ENCIRCLE	(A) crown	(B) grow from	10. _____
	(C) surround	(D) block	

11. INDECISIVE   (A) certain   (B) inflexible   11. _____
(C) intolerant   (D) unsure

12. TABOO   (A) forbidden   (B) modern   12. _____
(C) stylish   (D) unfashionable

13. TEMPERATE   (A) hot   (B) moderate   13. _____
(C) cold   (D) breezy

14. BON VOYAGE   (A) excuse me   (B) please   14. _____
(C) good journey   (D) good night

15. IMMODERATE   (A) bold   (B) embarrassed   15. _____
(C) above normal   (D) long

Part 2 Matching Words and Meanings

Match the definition in Column B with the word in Column A. Write
the letter of the correct definition on the line provided.

Column A   **Column B**

16. menagerie   a. muddled   16. _____

17. impenetrable   b. not loud enough to be heard   17. _____

18. frigid   c. unreachable   18. _____

19. uninhabitable   d. undeveloped   19. _____

20. inaccessible   e. collection of animals   20. _____

21. à la carte   f. priced per dish   21. _____

22. inaudible   g. unfit to be lived in   22. _____

23. array   h. impossible to pass through   23. _____

24. immature   i. cold, freezing   24. _____

25. incoherent   j. display   25. _____

Name _____

Arachne, the Weaver
–a Greek Myth

Arachne lived with her father, an **artisan** famous for the beautiful dyes he used to color his fine wools. At a young age, she had learned to spin her father's wool into a **delicate**, soft thread and to weave the thread into the finest cloth.

5   As Arachne grew, so did her skills. Each piece of cloth she wove was more beautiful than the last. She soon earned a **reputation** as the finest weaver in all of Greece. People traveled for miles just to watch her skillful hands create fine, colorful cloth. Even the nymphs of the forests would sometimes **lurk** about the windows of her cot-

10 tage, hoping to catch a glimpse of Arachne's talented hands at work.

Before long, however, people began to whisper, "No human could have taught her to spin the thread and weave it into such magnificent cloth. Athena, the goddess of wisdom and art, must have taught her."

15 Such talk made Arachne angry. One day, she could stand it no longer. "I learned my skills through long days and nights of practice," she said. "Athena is no match for my skills."

The crowd was stunned. Finally an old woman spoke up. "You fool! You must ask Athena's forgiveness for such a remark."

20 "Never!" snapped Arachne. "I challenge Athena to answer my words by **participating** in a contest to prove just who is the most skillful."

Before Arachne could finish her challenge, the old woman **transformed** herself into a tall, beautiful woman dressed in flow-

25 ing white robes. Everyone knew immediately that the old woman was Athena herself. Arachne was momentarily shaken but soon recovered. She would not **retract** her challenge.

The two approached a pair of looms and began to weave the colorful wool into cloth. For a few moments their skills seemed

30 equal, but gradually Athena moved ahead. **Infuriated** at the thought of losing, Arachne began to weave pictures of evil things gods had done to people. Athena answered this **impertinence** by grabbing Arachne and saying, "You and all your descendants shall spin, and your spinning will remind people never to compete with the gods."

35 At that Arachne **shriveled** into a small brown spider with six thin legs. She hung from one of the fine threads on her loom. All spiders are descended from Arachne, and their webs are a reminder that no mortal is equal to the gods.

Words

artisan

delicate

impertinence

infuriated

lurk

participate

reputation

retract

shrivel

transform

Each word in this lesson's word list appears in dark type in the selection you just read. Think about how the vocabulary word is used in the selection, then write the letter for the best answer to each question.

1. An *artisan* (line 1) can best be described as a _____.
   (A) rebellious citizen
   (B) strict parent
   (C) skilled craftsperson
   (D) friend of the gods

   1. _____

2. The word *delicate* (line 3) means _____.
   (A) fine in texture
   (B) tight-fitting
   (C) thick
   (D) sticky

   2. _____

3. Your *reputation* (line 6) is _____.
   (A) the knowledge you possess
   (B) your secret knowledge of others
   (C) your beliefs about the gods
   (D) the judgment others make of you

   3. _____

4. Another word for *lurk* (line 9) is _____.
   (A) sneak
   (B) play
   (C) fight
   (D) laugh

   4. _____

5. If you *participate* (line 21) in a contest, you _____.
   (A) decide the winner
   (B) take part in it
   (C) watch it as it occurs
   (D) ignore it

   5. _____

6. If you *transform* (line 24) something, you _____.
   (A) move it from place to place
   (B) copy it
   (C) change its form or appearance
   (D) make it invisible

   6. _____

7. The word *retract* in line 27 could best be replaced with _____.
   (A) explain
   (B) take back
   (C) repeat
   (D) change

   7. _____

8. Another word for *infuriated* (line 30) is _____.
   (A) surprised
   (B) amused
   (C) comforted
   (D) enraged

   8. _____

9. *Impertinence* (line 32) can best be described as _____.
   (A) compliments
   (B) clever remarks
   (C) rude behavior
   (D) impossible dreams

   9. _____

10. If something *shrivels* (line 35), it _____.
    (A) shrinks to a smaller size
    (B) makes loud noises
    (C) frightens away its enemies
    (D) dies

    10. _____

Applying Meaning

Follow the directions below to write a sentence using a-vocabulary word.

1. Describe a school activity. Use any form of the word *participate*.

   _____

   _____

   _____

2. Use *reputation* in a sentence about a political candidate.

   _____

   _____

   _____

3. Use any form of the word *retract* to describe what a newspaper did after it published a story.

   _____

   _____

   _____

4. Describe a scene from a horror movie. Use any form of the word *lurk*.

   _____

   _____

   _____

5. Use the word *delicate* to describe something you own or would like to own.

   _____

   _____

   _____

Each question below contains a vocabulary word from this lesson. Answer each question "yes" or "no" in the space provided.

6. Does an *artisan* treat diseases of the arteries?   6. _____

7. Would the sun *shrivel* a grape?   7. _____

8. Do most parents encourage *impertinence* from their children?   8. _____

9. When the clock struck midnight, was Cinderella's carriage *transformed* into a pumpkin?

9. _____

10. Would you want to *infuriate* your teacher the day he grades your test paper?

10. _____

For each question you answered "no," write a sentence explaining your reason.

_____

_____

_____

_____

_____

_____

_____

_____

_____

Mastering Meaning

The Greeks told myths like the story of Arachne to explain the world around them. Make up a story to explain one of the following. Use some of the words you studied in this lesson.

Why the leaves change color in the fall

Why thunder always follows lightning

Why bears sleep through the winter

Why the giraffe has a long neck

Name _____

Do you know someone who is brilliant at mathematics but can never remember where he put his coat? Do you know a football superstar who has trouble changing a light bulb? People are a complicated mixture of strengths and weaknesses. Our language, therefore, has many words to identify or describe them. In this lesson you will learn 10 such words.

Unlocking Meaning

Words

capable

defect

deficient

effectual

fallible

fault

feeble

potent

vigor

vulnerable

Read the sentences or short passages below. Write the letter for the correct definition of the italicized word.

1. It took weeks to find a *capable* carpenter willing to repair the damaged porch.
   (A) wealthy   (B) important
   (C) able   (D) well-known

2. The automobile dealer offered to correct the *defect* in the paint.
   (A) type of color   (B) value
   (C) blemish   (D) curve

3. A review of Julie's eating habits showed that her diet was *deficient* in vitamin C.
   (A) overly supplied   (B) suffering
   (C) absorbed   (D) lacking

1. _____

4. Firsthand experience on a boat is the only *effectual* way to learn how to sail.
   (A) truly effective   (B) educated
   (C) unlikely   (D) unhealthy

2. _____

5. Computers are not perfect. After all, they are built by *fallible* human beings.
   (A) intelligent   (B) able to make mistakes
   (C) illegal   (D) expert

3. _____

6. The only serious *fault* in the new play is its unlikely ending.
   (A) review   (B) error
   (C) appeal   (D) explanation

4. _____

5. _____

6. _____

7. The last-minute try at scoring a field goal was a *feeble* attempt by our team to avoid being held scoreless.

    (A) weak   (B) silent

    (C) heroic   (D) foolish

7. _____

8. The speaker gave *potent* examples of waste and corruption in several government programs.

    (A) unusual   (B) unconvincing

    (C) exaggerated   (D) powerful

8. _____

9. The *vigor* Jean showed in practice convinced Coach Swanson to start her in the next game.

    (A) energy or strength   (B) absent-mindedness

    (C) intelligence   (D) lack of interest

9. _____

10. Unless you get a shot in the fall, you will be *vulnerable* to the flu when winter arrives.

    (A) valued   (B) impossible to touch

    (C) easily harmed   (D) hidden

10. _____

Each question below contains one or more vocabulary words from the lesson. Answer each question "yes" or "no" in the space provided.

1. Would you want an *effectual* surgeon to repair a *defect* in your heart?

2. Does an employer try to hire as many *deficient* workers as possible?

3. Are children more *vulnerable* to measles and mumps than adults are?

4. Did the wicked witch give Snow White a magic *potent*?

5. Would a *fault* in the rocket engine cause a delay in a space mission?

1. _____

2. _____

3. _____

4. _____

5. _____

For each question you answered "no," write a sentence explaining your reason.

_____

_____

_____

_____

_____

_____

_____

_____

_____

_____

Decide which word in parentheses best completes the sentence. Then write the sentence, adding the missing word.

6. In spite of his many accomplishments, Lincoln was still a _____ human being. (capable; fallible)

_____

_____

_____

7. Behind by 30 points, the team had lost the _____ and enthusiasm it showed when the game started. (fault; vigor)

_____

_____

_____

8. Although Matt got a B on his essay, his teacher felt he was _____ of better work. (capable; fallible)

_____

_____

_____

9. The candidate's reminder about his war record was a _____ effort to avoid answering the question. (capable; feeble)

_____

_____

_____

10. If students have not been taught to use a computer, their education is _____ in an important area. (deficient; potent)

_____

_____

_____

Bonus Word

gadfly

The term *gadfly* originally referred to several varieties of large, stinging flies, such as the common horsefly. Such flies would sting cattle, horses, and other livestock. Over time the term was applied to a person who is a persistent source of annoyance or a general nuisance. This is not necessarily a negative term. Some "gadflies," like Martin Luther King, Jr., have brought about important changes.

Cooperative Learning: Work with a partner to make a list of positive and negative gadflies in American history.

Lesson

30

Part A

Name _____

Most words can be changed from one part of speech to another through the simple addition of a suffix. Some words, however, change in more basic ways. As a result, two words that appear to be quite different from one another can actually be related to each other in meaning. In this lesson you will study five such pairs of words with related meanings.

Unlocking Meaning

Each short passage below contains two italicized words that are related in meaning. Read each passage and think about how the words are used. Then write the letters for the correct answers to the questions.

The police will *detain* the suspect for 24 hours. He will be held in *detention* in the county jail.

1. To *detain* is to _____.
   - (A) keep from leaving
   - (B) tear apart
   - (C) annoy
   - (D) help

2. Another word for *detention* is _____.
   - (A) explanation
   - (B) confinement
   - (C) courtesy
   - (D) peace.

Even though we were leading by a touchdown, I *doubted* that we could hold the lead. After seeing our team lose the last three games in the final quarter, most of us were still *dubious* about the outcome of the game.

3 To *doubt* is to _____.
   - (A) avoid people
   - (B) offer excuses
   - (C) lose interest
   - (D) be uncertain

4 A *dubious* plan is _____.
   - (A) well liked
   - (B) unlikely to succeed
   - (C) one created by an expert
   - (D) borrowed from another source

Words

- **detain**
- **detention**
- **doubt**
- **dubious**
- **invocation**
- **invoke**
- **remain**
- **remnant**
- **require**
- **requisite**

1. _____

2. _____

3. _____

4. _____

After months of drought, the tribal leaders decided to *invoke* the help of the gods. Their *invocation* took the form of an elaborate ceremony of dance, music, and incantations.

5. If you invoke someone, you _____.
   (A) threaten him   (B) amuse him
   (C) ask for his or her help   (D) answer his question

5. _____

6. An *invocation* is a(n) _____.
   (A) invention   (B) type of religion
   (C) appeal   (D) magic trick

6. _____

All that *remains* of the ancient temple are a few stones and the foundation. Yet from these *remnants* it is possible for the experts to reconstruct the original building.

7. To *remain* is to _____.
   (A) taste   (B) stay behind
   (C) put in a straight line   (D) deliver

7. _____

8. A *remnant* is _____.
   (A) what is left over   (B) money paid for rent
   (C) a loud speech   (D) a four-sided figure

8. _____

Skiing down Mount Killington *requires* a high degree of skill. *Requisite* instruction on the various trails and weather conditions is provided every day.

9. Another word for *require* is _____.
   (A) desire   (B) repeat
   (C) release   (D) demand

9. _____

10. *Requisite* instruction is _____.
    (A) unnecessary   (B) essential
    (C) difficult   (D) playful

10. _____

Applying Meaning

Read each sentence below. Write "correct" on the answer line if the vocabulary word has been used correctly or "incorrect" if it has been used incorrectly.

1. Wearing a hairnet and an apron are *requisites* for working in the school kitchen.

2. Mrs. Molla kept Josh and me after school. We served our *detention* in the library.

3. We all tried very hard not to laugh, but Max's imitation of the principal was so *dubious* we couldn't help it.

4. She is studying anatomy and chemistry because she hopes to pursue an *invocation* in medicine.

5. The farmer reported that a large silver disk with flashing lights had landed in his field. We all felt it was a *remnant* of his imagination.

1. _____

2. _____

3. _____

4. _____

5. _____

For each word used incorrectly, write a sentence using the word properly.

_____

_____

_____

_____

_____

_____

_____

_____

Follow the directions below to write a sentence using a vocabulary word.

6. Use any form of the word *doubt* in a sentence about the outcome of a baseball or basketball game.

_____

_____

_____

7. Write a sentence explaining why you or someone else was late for an important event. Use any form of the word *detain*.

_____

_____

_____

8. Use any form of the word *require* in a sentence about joining a team, club, or organization.

_____

_____

_____

9. Write a sentence about the life or religious practices of an ancient people. Use any form of the word *invoke*.

_____

_____

_____

10. Use any form of the word *remain* in a sentence about the results of a fire or storm.

_____

_____

_____

Test-Taking Strategies

Tests of reading comprehension ask you to read one or two selections and answer some questions to test how well you have understood what you read. The questions often ask you to draw inferences from the information. For example, if someone sees his breath when he exhales, we can infer that he is outside during winter.

Reread the selection *Matthew Henson, Arctic Explorer* on page 99. Write an X next to the statements that might be inferred from this essay.

1. The ship's library had books on navigation.   1. _____

2. Inuit is a difficult language to learn.   2. _____

3. Civil engineers in 1908 had personal attendants.   3. _____

4. Henson was less affected by the cold conditions at the North Pole than Peary was.   4. _____

Name _____

How well do you remember the words you studied in Lessons 28 through 30? Take the following test covering the words from the last three lessons.

Part 1 Choose the Correct Meaning

Each question below includes a word in capital letters, followed by four words or phrases. Choose the word or phrase that is <u>closest</u> in meaning to the word in capital letters. Write the letter for your answer on the line provided.

Sample

S. FINISH	(A) enjoy	(B) complete	S. _____
	(C) destroy	(D) enlarge	

1. DEFICIENT	(A) unskilled	(B) rich	1. _____
	(C) slow	(D) lacking	
2. ARTISAN	(A) craftsperson	(B) collector	2. _____
	(C) teacher	(D) writer	
3. LURK	(A) sing	(B) climb	3. _____
	(C) prowl	(D) work	
4. REQUISITE	(A) necessary	(B) multiple	4. _____
	(C) old	(D) fragile	
5. POTENT	(A) bitter	(B) smelly	5. _____
	(C) strong	(D) sweet	
6. VIGOR	(A) skill	(B) fondness	6. _____
	(C) speed	(D) energy	
7. SHRIVEL	(A) shrink	(B) smell	7. _____
	(C) lose color	(D) come undone	
8. PARTICIPATE	(A) engage in	(B) talk about	8. _____
	(C) think about	(D) consider	
9. FEEBLE	(A) new	(B) admirable	9. _____
	(C) reckless	(D) weak	
10. INFURIATED	(A) surprised	(B) angered	10. _____
	(C) threatened	(D) delighted	

11. VULNERABLE   (A) resistant   (B) cured   11. _____

                    (C) unprotected   (D) prepared

12. CAPABLE   (A) known for   (B) ready   12. _____

                    (C) guilty   (D) able

13. DELICATE   (A) fine   (B) old   13. _____

                    (C) colorful   (D) attractive

14. RETRACT   (A) repeat   (B) change   14. _____

                    (C) translate   (D) take back

15. IMPERTINENCE   (A) rudeness   (B) success   15. _____

                    (C) laughter   (D) daring

Part 2 Matching Words and Meanings

Match the definition in Column B with the word in Column A. Write the letter of the correct definition on the line provided.

Column A	**Column B**	
16. detain	a. change	16. _____
17. detention	b. remainder	17. _____
18. transform	c. hold back	18. _____
19. defect	d. plead	19. _____
20. doubt	e. request	20. _____
21. dubious	f. fault	21. _____
22. invocation	g. be unsure	22. _____
23. invoke	h. unlikely	23. _____
24. fallible	i. able to make mistakes	24. _____
25. remnant	j. confinement	25. _____

Name _____

Great Tombs

Over the course of history, civilizations have **entombed** their dead in various ways. Two of the most impressive tombs are the Taj Mahal and the Great Pyramid. The Taj Mahal was erected by the emperor Shah Jahan as a **mausoleum** for his dead wife. Twenty
5 thousand workers toiled for nearly 20 years to build the white marble structure. The jeweled building seems to float on the banks of the Jumna River in Agra, India. This domed building is laid out in perfectly balanced elements.

The Taj Mahal's white marble **facade** stands in distinct contrast
10 to the red sandstone fronts of the surrounding buildings. The architectural **ingenuity** of its design can also be seen in the carved marble screens at the tops of the walls. Not only do these furnish additional beauty, but the sunlight that passes through them provides **illumination** for the interior of the building. This magnifi-
15 cent structure is commonly acknowledged as one of the world's most beautiful buildings and an architectural masterpiece.

In ancient Egypt, deceased **pharaohs** and their families were laid to rest in pyramids. The Great Pyramid at Giza is the largest of these. Cheops, who ruled Egypt from 2590 to 2567 B.C., forced
20 nearly every man in Egypt to work on his massive tomb.

Built when machinery did not exist, this mammoth structure of stone represents a tremendous **feat** of engineering. Nearly 2.5 million stone blocks, weighing over 5,000 pounds each, make up the Great Pyramid. Lacking written records of the construction,
25 scholars can only speculate as to how the laborers moved these monstrous weights. One theory holds that as each level was constructed, a spiral ramp was built to **convey** stones to the next levels. Upon completion, a **gilded** stone was placed at the pyramid's **pinnacle** during an elaborate ceremony. Once this golden marker
30 was in place, workers trimmed the stones and applied a limestone facing.

Today the Great Pyramid lacks its original outer facing of limestone. Over the centuries, the limestone was stripped to provide building materials for the nearby city of Cairo.

Words
convey
entomb
facade
feat
gilded
illumination
ingenuity
mausoleum
pharaoh
pinnacle

Each word in this lesson's word list appears in dark type in the selection you just read. Think about how the vocabulary word is used in the selection. Then write the letter for the best answer to each question.

1. To *entomb* (line 1) is to _____.
   (A) sing about
   (B) dishonor or disgrace
   (C) place in a grave or chamber
   (D) make angry

1. _____

2. A *mausoleum* (line 4) is a _____.
   (A) building housing a tomb
   (B) prison
   (C) type of museum
   (D) plastic covering

2. _____

3. A *facade* (line 9) is a _____.
   (A) steep hill
   (B) front of a building
   (C) series of small waterfalls
   (D) ceiling or wall of a cave

3. _____

4 Another word for *ingenuity* (line 11) is _____.
   (A) carelessness
   (B) importance
   (C) curiosity
   (D) creativity

4. _____

5. If something provides *illumination* (line 14), it provides _____.
   (A) a type of conflict
   (B) an opportunity for escape
   (C) a source of light
   (D) protection from fire

5. _____

6. A *pharaoh* (line 17) was a(n) _____.
   (A) farmer in Egypt
   (B) ancient Egyptian slave
   (C) Egyptian outlaw
   (D) king of ancient Egypt

6. _____

7. Which word could best replace *feat* in line 22?
   (A) achievement
   (B) insult
   (C) failure
   (D) denial

7. _____

8. To *convey* (line 27) is to _____.
   (A) discuss
   (B) move or carry
   (C) attack
   (D) decrease

8. _____

9. Something that is *gilded* (line 28) is _____.
   (A) floating silently
   (B) fake
   (C) godlike
   (D) covered with a layer of gold

9. _____

10. The *pinnacle* (line 29) of something is its _____.
    (A) center
    (B) lowest point
    (C) highest point
    (D) outer surface

10. _____

Name _____

Applying Meaning

Follow the directions below to write a sentence using a vocabulary word.

1. Describe a great accomplishment. Use the word *feat*.

   _____

   _____

   _____

2. Write a sentence about a horror movie. Use a form of the word *entomb* in your sentence.

   _____

   _____

   _____

3. Use the word *pinnacle* to describe a mountain climbing expedition.

   _____

   _____

   _____

4. Describe a building. Use the word *facade*.

   _____

   _____

   _____

5. Write a sentence about ancient Egypt. Use the word *pharaoh* in your sentence.

   _____

   _____

   _____

Each question below contains a vocabulary word from this lesson. Answer the question "yes" or "no" in the space provided.

6. If you were stranded on an island, would some *ingenuity* come in handy?

   6. _____

7. Could a candle provide *illumination* during a power outage?

   7. _____

8. Would you expect to find *gilded* items in the humble cottage of a poor peasant?

   8. _____

9. Might troops of soldiers be *conveyed* to a foreign region in military aircraft?

9. _____

10. Would a zoologist visit a *mausoleum* to study animals?

10. _____

For each question you answered "no," write a sentence explaining your reason.

_____

_____

_____

_____

_____

_____

_____

_____

Mastering Meaning

The Great Pyramids of Egypt are among the Seven Wonders of the Ancient World. Select a monument, structure, or site in the modern world that you think is a wonder of beauty or engineering. Write a paragraph explaining why you believe your choice should be named a Modern Wonder of the World. You might consider the Empire State Building, Mount Rushmore, the Eiffel Tower, the Golden Gate Bridge, the Statue of Liberty, the Sistine Chapel, London Bridge, or the Gateway Arch in Saint Louis.

Name _____

People communicate mostly through speaking and writing. Depending on the circumstances, we use varying forms and methods to communicate. The English language abounds with words associated with various ways of speaking and writing. In this lesson you will learn 10 of these words.

Unlocking Meaning

A vocabulary word appears in italics in each sentence or short passage below. Think about how the word is used in the passage. Then write a definition for the vocabulary word. Compare your definition with the definition in the dictionary in the back of the book.

Words
banal
boisterous
clamor
coax
dialogue
draft
endorse
platitude
recant
scrawl

1. After an hour of *banal* conversation on the weather and sports, I nearly fell asleep.

   _____

   _____

   _____

2. The team could not hear the plays being called by the quarterback over the *boisterous* hometown crowd.

   _____

   _____

   _____

3. When the tax bills arrived, there was a public *clamor* for a repeal of the increased taxes.

   _____

   _____

   _____

4. It took hours to *coax* my frightened kitten down from the tree.

   _____

   _____

   _____

5. We hoped an informal meeting would lead to a *dialogue* between union and management before a strike began.

   _____

   _____

   _____

6. The teacher insisted we write a *draft* of our essays and revise it before handing it in.

   _____

   _____

   _____

7. If the mayor and city council *endorse* the park plan, it will be much easier to get a government grant for the project.

   _____

   _____

   _____

8. I refuse to support a candidate who speaks in *platitudes*. Just what does he mean by "I'm for progress"?

   _____

   _____

   _____

9. After a recount showed he had won the election, Senator Case had to *recant* his statement that the election was fixed.

   _____

   _____

   _____

10. As I rushed out the door, I was able to *scrawl* a short note to Ellie so she would know where I had gone.

    _____

    _____

    _____

Applying Meaning

Decide which word in parentheses best completes the sentence. Then write the sentence, adding the missing word.

1. Vandals had _____ their names in spray paint all over the wooden barriers along the highway. (endorsed; scrawled)

   _____

   _____

   _____

2. Critics raved about the snappy _____ between the two comic characters in the film. (dialogue; platitude)

   _____

   _____

   _____

3. The former governor claimed he was neutral and refused to _____ any candidate. (coax; endorse)

   _____

   _____

   _____

4. Her advisors suggested she fill her speech with _____ that everyone could agree to without offending anyone. (drafts; platitudes)

   _____

   _____

   _____

5. Theo tried to _____ the parrot onto his finger, but the bird would not leave its perch. (coax; scrawl)

   _____

   _____

   _____

6. We had to turn in a first _____ of the report by Friday. The final report was due a week later. (dialogue; draft)

   _____

   _____

   _____

Each question below contains a vocabulary word from this lesson.
Answer the question "yes" or "no" in the space provided.

7. Is a *banal* worn around the neck?

7. _____

8. Would a group of *boisterous* students be welcome in the library?

8. _____

9. Would a journalist want to *recant* a statement that she knows to be accurate?

9. _____

10. Could the *clamor* from a party next door keep you awake at night?

10. _____

For each question you answered "no," write a sentence explaining your reason.

_____

_____

_____

_____

_____

_____

_____

_____

Bonus Word

hubbub

The English word *hubbub,* meaning "loud noise," may have its source in *ub ub ubub,* a Gaelic expression of contempt, or *abu,* an Irish war cry. In either case it may have been borrowed by the English as a term of disdain for people of Celtic origins. In colonial America the term was used to describe a noisy game played by the Native American inhabitants.

Use a Thesaurus: There are many words in the English language that describe the sounds we make. Use a thesaurus to find at least five words for noises. Be prepared to explain how the meaning of each word differs from the others.

Name _____

The prefix *dis-* appears at the beginning of many English words or roots. Its most common meanings are "not," "opposite of," or "undo." The prefix *dis-* comes from the Latin preposition *dis*, meaning "apart" or "asunder." All of the words in this lesson begin with the prefix *dis-*.

Prefix	Word or Root	Word
dis-	engage	disengage
dis-	tort	distort

Unlocking Meaning

A vocabulary word appears in italics in each passage below. Think about how the word is used in the passage. Then write a definition for the vocabulary word. Compare your definition with the definition in the dictionary at the back of the book.

1. When the police officers arrived, they acted quickly to *disarm* the fugitive. His gun was kept as evidence.

   _____

   _____

   _____

2. The books and papers on my desk were in total *disarray*. It took me an hour to find what I was looking for.

   _____

   _____

   _____

3. If anyone asks, I will *disavow* any knowledge of Ed's whereabouts. He needs some time to study for the exam.

   _____

   _____

   _____

4. I will *disclaim* any right to an inheritance from my aunt's estate.

   _____

   _____

   _____

Words

disarm

disarray

disavow

disclaim

disclose

discredit

disengage

disheveled

disillusion

distort

5. The prosecutor will *disclose* the evidence during the trial.

   _____

   _____

   _____

6. Evidence in recent fossil discoveries seems to *discredit* earlier theories that life could not exist on Mars.

   _____

   _____

   _____

7. After the supplies are unloaded, the space shuttle will *disengage* from the space station and return to earth.

   _____

   _____

   _____

8. The wind and rain gave her a *disheveled* appearance when she arrived at work.

   _____

   _____

   _____

9. After finding no gold after months of digging, many of the forty-niners became *disillusioned* and returned to the East.

   _____

   _____

   _____

10. The senator accused the candidate of trying to *distort* the facts on unemployment in order to gain votes.

   _____

   _____

   _____

Applying Meaning

Decide which word in parentheses best completes the sentence. Then write the sentence, adding the missing word.

1. The victorious army immediately began to _____ the defeated troops and its civilian supporters. (disarm; distort)

_____

_____

_____

2. You should never _____ information such as your social security number over the telephone. (disclose; discredit)

_____

_____

_____

3. After the party, our apartment was in a state of total _____. (disarray; disclosure)

_____

_____

_____

4. Standing on the windswept beach, the _____ reporter updated viewers on the hurricane. (disarmed; disheveled)

_____

_____

_____

5. The face I had drawn on the balloon became _____ when the balloon was inflated. (disclaimed; distorted)

_____

_____

_____

6. Would it _____ you to learn that the rock star is only pretending to play the guitar? (disavow; disillusion)

_____

_____

_____

7. The witness's testimony was _____ when two neighbors said he was with them at the time. (discredited; disheveled)

_____

_____

_____

8. Knowing he did not deserve the award, he _____ any right to it. (disclaimed; disengaged)

_____

_____

_____

9. She _____ herself from the club when she learned it denied membership to certain minorities. (disengaged; disillusioned)

_____

_____

_____

10. The suspect firmly _____ any knowledge of the scheme to overcharge customers. (disarrayed; disavowed)

_____

_____

_____

Using the Dictionary

Dictionaries provide information on the inflected forms of words.

The plural, -ed, and -ing forms of the entry word are usually given immediately following the entry word. Some more advanced dictionaries may list only the irregularly inflected forms of the entry word.

be•gin (bī gĭn′), v., **be•gan**, **be•gun**, **be•gin•ning**. **1.** to start. **2.** to come into being.

Look up the following words in a dictionary. List the inflected forms for each word. Use one of the inflected forms in a sentence.

leave   prefer   relate   buy   give

How well do you remember the words you studied in Lessons 31 through 33? Take the following test covering the words from the last three lessons.

Part 1 Choose the Correct Meaning

Each question below includes a word in capital letters, followed by four words or phrases. Choose the word or phrase that is <u>closest</u> in meaning to the word in capital letters. Write the letter for your answer on the line provided.

Sample

S. FINISH	(A) enjoy (C) destroy	(B) complete (D) enlarge	S. _____
1 FACADE	(A) weapon (C) fake	(B) surface (D) assistance	1. _____
2. DISENGAGE	(A) detach (C) embrace	(B) destroy (D) collect	2. _____
3. COAX	(A) split (C) put in order	(B) join together (D) urge	3. _____
4. INGENUITY	(A) curiosity (C) disguise	(B) storyteller (D) creativity	4. _____
5. DISARRAY	(A) confusion (C) misuse	(B) fashionable clothing (D) urgent request	5. _____
6. BANAL	(A) hidden (C) dull	(B) lengthy (D) scholarly	6. _____
7. GILDED	(A) disgusting (C) opened	(B) decorated (D) easily tricked	7. _____
8. PLATITUDE	(A) pleasing attitude (C) common remark	(B) command (D) height	8. _____
9. DISHEVELED	(A) rumpled (C) disappointed	(B) broken (D) foolish	9. _____
10. ENDORSE	(A) understand (C) toss aside	(B) approve (D) reject	10. _____

11. RECANT   (A) release   (B) surrender   11. _____

                (C) avoid   (D) take back

12. PINNACLE   (A) pointed   (B) wound   12. _____

                (C) peak   (D) type of cloth

13. ENTOMB   (A) bury   (B) turn over   13. _____

                (C) pull apart   (D) mislead

14. DISCLAIM   (A) call out   (B) deny   14. _____

                (C) take possession of   (D) divide

15. DISTORT   (A) change shape   (B) judge   15. _____

                (C) remove   (D) straighten

Part 2 Matching Words and Meanings

Match the definition in Column B with the word in Column A. Write the letter of the correct definition on the line provided.

Column A	Column B	
16. feat	a. cause to lose faith in a belief	16. _____
17. draft	b. conversation	17. _____
18. dialogue	c. deny	18. _____
19. illumination	d. achievement	19. _____
20. boisterous	e. loud	20. _____
21. disclose	f. initial plan	21. _____
22. disillusion	g. stately tomb	22. _____
23. convey	h. reveal	23. _____
24. mausoleum	i. transport	24. _____
25. disavow	j. light	25. _____

Name _____

Inventors and Inventions

Turn on the TV with the remote control. Open a can. Telephone
a friend. Dim the lights. Listen to a CD. Switch on the computer.
Do just about anything, and you are **reaping** the benefits of the
innovative minds of inventors. Inventors are a remarkable **breed**.
5 They may look like your next-door neighbors and could, in fact,
even be your neighbors. However, research has shown that most
inventors possess **distinctive** characteristics that separate them
from the general population.

When faced with complex problems, inventors employ creative
10 techniques to find solutions. Not surprisingly, this **trait** makes them
superb problem solvers. They often have broad interests and do
not usually limit themselves to one area of **expertise**. They are
inquisitive and self-motivated, always eager to investigate the
"whys" and "hows" of things. Inventors are also doers; they **strive**
15 to complete tasks, driven primarily by the need to know the final
results.

Inventors display a strong work ethic. They remain committed to
a task, **persistent** and determined to see it through to a final resolu-
tion. When trying to solve problems, they are not easily discouraged,
20 are willing to consider the advice of others, and often use both tradi-
tional and experimental approaches to find solutions. Inventors generally have several hobbies and are likely to **embrace** them with the
same enthusiasm and vigor they apply to their work.

You have probably studied famous inventors such as Alexander
25 Graham Bell (telephone); Thomas Edison (microphone and phono-
graph); Orville and Wilbur Wright (motorized airplane); George
Washington Carver (agricultural techniques); and Henry Ford (assembly line). Their inventions revolutionized the world.

However, you should not forget the contributions of other equally
30 important inventors. Although their names are not household words,
their inventions have permanently altered how we work, play, and
live. They include Alexander Cartwright (baseball), Whitcomb
Judson (the zipper), Gertrude Elion (cancer treatment drugs), and
Carl Benz and Otto Daimler (gasoline automobile).

Words

breed

distinctive

embrace

expertise

innovative

inquisitive

persistent

reap

strive

trait

Each word in this lesson's word list appears in dark type in the selection you just read. Think about how the vocabulary word is used in the selection. Then write the letter for the best answer to each question.

1. The word *reaping* in line 3 means _____.
   (A) looking at   (B) preparing
   (C) stealing   (D) receiving as a reward

   1. _____

2. An *innovative* (line 4) mind can best be described as one that is _____.
   (A) easily confused   (B) odd but harmless
   (C) a source of new ideas   (D) subject to sudden changes

   2. _____

3. Which word could best replace *breed* in line 4?
   (A) type   (B) grain
   (C) sight   (D) design

   3. _____

4. A *distinctive* (line 7) characteristic is _____.
   (A) distasteful to others   (B) natural
   (C) set apart from others   (D) hidden from view

   4. _____

5. Another word for *trait* (line 10) is _____.
   (A) complication   (B) feature
   (C) course   (D) job

   5. _____

6. If you have *expertise* (line 12) in an area, you have _____.
   (A) know-how   (B) money
   (C) questions   (D) ignorance

   6. _____

7. To be *inquisitive* (line 13) is to be _____.
   (A) unfeeling   (B) lazy
   (C) disinterested   (D) curious

   7. _____

8. Which phrase could best replace *strive* in line 14?
   (A) walk quickly and purposefully   (B) try hard
   (C) work carelessly   (D) refuse repeatedly

   8. _____

9. A *persistent* (line 18) person could best be described as someone who _____.
   (A) surrenders quickly   (B) is annoying
   (C) refuses to give up   (D) treats others badly

   9. _____

10. To *embrace* (line 22) a hobby is to _____.
    (A) limit it   (B) eagerly engage in it
    (C) eliminate it   (D) confuse it with something else

    10. _____

Applying Meaning

Follow the directions below to write a sentence using a vocabulary word.

1. Write a sentence about a successful teacher. Use the word *innovative* in your sentence.

   _____

   _____

   _____

2. Describe how a particular food tastes. Use the word *distinctive*.

   _____

   _____

   _____

3. Describe the character of a person you admire. Use the word *trait*.

   _____

   _____

   _____

4. Use any form of the word *persistent* in a sentence about a salesperson.

   _____

   _____

   _____

5. Write a sentence about a well-known person in history. Use the word *inquisitive*.

   _____

   _____

   _____

6. Use the word *breed* to describe a group of musicians.

   _____

   _____

   _____

7. Describe the work of an activist for a particular cause. Use any form of the word *strive*.

_____

_____

_____

8. Describe a chef. Use the word *expertise*.

_____

_____

_____

9. Write a sentence about the consequences of someone's actions. Use any form of the word *reap*.

_____

_____

_____

10. Use any form of the word *embrace* to describe someone who has recently moved from the city to the country.

_____

_____

_____

Mastering Meaning

As the head of a major research and development company, you are seeking to hire several inventors to develop new products for your company. Write a Help Wanted advertisement describing the kind of people you are seeking to fill these positions. Use some of the words you have studied in this lesson.

Vocabulary of Smell and Taste

Name _____

Have you ever wondered what it would be like to be a food critic? Food critics do not just review the food they eat; they describe the total dining experience. This kind of descriptive writing relies on words that convey the sensory experience of dining, especially words associated with taste and smell. In this lesson, you will learn 10 words related to taste and smell.

Unlocking Meaning

Read the sentences or short passages below. Write the letter for the correct definition of the italicized vocabulary word.

1. I was not hungry when I sat down, but the food brought to the table was so *appetizing* that I could not wait to eat.
   (A) lacking in flavor   (B) colorful
   (C) creating a desire for food (D) having an offensive odor

2. The *aromas* coming from the kitchen made my mouth water.
   (A) pleasant smells   (B) odd noises
   (C) smoky appearance   (D) sickening odors

3. The food critic stated that a fine restaurant should offer a choice of several *delectable* main courses.
   (A) expensive   (B) uncooked or raw
   (C) mysterious   (D) very delicious

4. You can distinguish many herbs by their *fragrance* alone. Basil smells minty, while rosemary has a flowery scent.
   (A) shape   (B) size
   (C) sweet or pleasant odor   (D) strong, foul taste

5. The hot spices in the Indian food were so *pungent* that they made our eyes water.
   (A) extremely sweet tasting (B) bland or dull; tasteless
   (C) foreign or strange   (D) having a sharp or strong taste or smell

Words

appetizing

aroma

delectable

fragrance

pungent

reek

savor

stench

tart

whiff

1. _____

2. _____

3. _____

4. _____

5. _____

6. After the cook dropped the carton of rotten eggs, the kitchen *reeked* for days.

6. _____

    (A) gave off a strong, unpleasant odor   (B) appeared clean

    (C) became unsanitary   (D) gave off an appealing odor

7. I ate my meal slowly because I wanted to *savor* every single bite of the pizza.

7. _____

    (A) ignore the bad taste of   (B) describe

    (C) enjoy the taste or smell of   (D) cook or prepare in an oven

8. The *stench* coming from nearby garbage cans ruined our picnic in Jones Park.

8. _____

    (A) delightful flavor   (B) strong, foul scent

    (C) heavy smoke   (D) sugary taste

9. Without sugar or some sweetener this lemonade is too *tart* for my taste.

9. _____

    (A) spicy   (B) sweet

    (C) thick   (D) sour

10. When I opened the refrigerator, I got a *whiff* of something that told me that the meat had gone bad.

10. _____

    (A) brief, passing odor   (B) quick glimpse

    (C) sharp sound   (D) annoying feeling

Applying Meaning

Follow the directions below to write a sentence using a vocabulary word.

1. Describe a recent meal. Use the word *delectable*.

   _____

   _____

   _____

2. Use the word *stench* in a description of a body of water.

   _____

   _____

   _____

3. Write a sentence about a menu. Use the word *appetizing* in your sentence.

   _____

   _____

   _____

4. Describe a garden. Use any form of the word *fragrance*.

   _____

   _____

   _____

5. Write a sentence about pizza. Use the word *aroma* in your sentence.

   _____

   _____

   _____

Read each sentence below. Write "correct" on the answer line if the vocabulary word has been used correctly or "incorrect" if it has been used incorrectly.

6. I could barely smell the *pungent* odors coming from the food simmering on the stove.

   6. _____

7. The seafood-processing factory and wholesale market *reeked* of dead fish.

   7. _____

8. The recipe for the pie called for fresh *tart* cherries, not sweet ones.

   8. _____

9. Mom caught me just as I was popping a *whiff* of chocolate cake into my mouth before dinner.

9. _____

10. I never rush through dessert. I like to *savor* each morsel.

10. _____

For each word used incorrectly, write a sentence using the word properly.

_____

_____

_____

_____

_____

_____

_____

Our Living Language

The human tongue can detect four tastes: *sweet, sour, salty,* and *bitter.* In the English language, however, the use of these four words goes beyond just describing taste. A number of idioms, proverbs, and other expressions include one of these four words. For example, "to be sweet on" is an idiom meaning "to be fond of" or "in love with." Some of these expressions have interesting origins. For example, "to be worth one's salt," means "to be hardworking and efficient," or "worth one's wages." This expression comes from the Roman custom of paying soldiers with salt.

Cooperative Learning: With a partner, make a list of idioms, proverbs, and other expressions that contain the words *sweet, sour, salt* or *salty,* or *bitter.* You might list "a bitter pill to swallow," "sour grapes," or "salt of the earth." Write a brief explanation of the meaning for each expression.

Name _____

The prefix *com-* comes from the Latin *com-*, meaning "together" or "with." Things that are "combined" are mixed together. Before some words or roots this prefix is spelled *con-* or *col-*.

Root	Meaning	Word
com-	with, together	compromise
con-		conformity
col-		collaborate

Unlocking Meaning

A vocabulary word appears in italics in each passage below. The meaning of its root is given in parentheses. Look at the prefix and think about how the word is used in the passage. Then write a definition for the vocabulary word. Compare your definition with the dictionary definition at the back of the book.

1. Dr. Lee said he would *collaborate* with Dr. West on a book about their research. (Root word: *laborare,* "to work")

   _____

   _____

   _____

2. To copy and accurately *collate* all the pages in this long report will take hours. (Root word: *latum,* "brought")

   _____

   _____

   _____

3. On the Fourth of July we *commemorate* our country's independence with fireworks and parades. (Root word: *memorare,* "to remind")

   _____

   _____

   _____

Words

collaborate

collate

commemorate

commingle

compromise

concur

condolence

confide

confiscate

conformity

4. Let the stew simmer for several hours so the flavors of the ingredients will *commingle*. (Root word: *mengan,* "to mix")

_____

_____

_____

5. Both men claimed the land, but they agreed to a *compromise* and split it between them. (Root word: *promittere,* "to promise")

_____

_____

_____

6. The candidates differed on most issues, but they did *concur* on the need for clean air. (Root word: *currere,* "to run")

_____

_____

_____

7. It was very thoughtful of Willa to express her *condolences* to me when my dog died. (Root word: *dolere,* "to grieve")

_____

_____

_____

8. I decided to *confide* my secret to Ben because I knew he would not reveal it to anyone. (Root word: *fidere,* "to trust")

_____

_____

_____

9. The FBI has the power to *confiscate* the property of anyone suspected of selling drugs. (Root word: *fiscus,* "treasury")

_____

_____

_____

10. The uniforms were one means of ensuring *conformity* to the school dress code. (Root word: *formare,* "to shape")

_____

_____

_____

Applying Meaning

Read each sentence below. Write "correct" on the answer line if the vocabulary word has been used correctly or "incorrect" if it has been used incorrectly.

1. To *commemorate* the end of the war, a statue was erected at the site where the treaty was signed.

2. When asked about the frog's extra limbs, the scientist explained that toxic chemicals could have caused the *conformity*.

3. Between classes students *commingle* in the halls.

4. We must get the *condolence* of the owner before we drive our snowmobile over these fields.

5. After her conviction her lawyers asked that the judge not *confide* her to prison for more than 30 days.

1. _____

2. _____

3. _____

4. _____

5. _____

For each word used incorrectly, write a sentence using the word properly.

_____

_____

_____

_____

_____

_____

_____

Decide which word in parentheses best completes the sentence. Then write the sentence, adding the missing word.

6. Even though they may not _____ with the decisions of their commander, soldiers must carry out their orders. (collaborate; concur)

_____

_____

_____

7. Because Raoul is a good writer and Yolanda an excellent artist, they plan to _____ on children's book. (collaborate; compromise)

_____

_____

_____

8. The principal warned that teachers would _____ gum and other food items if they were eaten during class. (collaborate; confiscate)

_____

_____

_____

9. Ed's job is to _____ all the sections of the Sunday newspaper and wrap them for delivery. (collate; confide)

_____

_____

_____

10. The workers and management were able to reach a _____ in their dispute over wages and overtime. (compromise; conformity)

_____

_____

_____

Test-Taking Strategies

Sentence-completion tests ask you to select the best word or words to complete a sentence. Before selecting an answer, read each item carefully and eliminate the choices that are obviously incorrect. Then search for clues to the overall meaning of the sentence. Finally, try each of the possible answers in the sentence and choose the best one.

Practice: Choose the word or set of words that, when inserted into the sentence, best fits the meaning of the sentence.

1. Unfortunately, we arrived at the movie theater so late that tickets were _____ for the film we wanted to see.
   (A) ruined   (B) unavailable
   (C) furnished   (D) selected

   1. _____

2. It was a(n) _____ production, but the script was based on an existing play by William Shakespeare.
   (A) illegal   (B) terrifying
   (C) original   (D) unplanned

   2. _____

3. This _____ program combines a healthy diet with daily _____.
   (A) scholastic . . . exams   (B) scientific . . . outbursts
   (C) outdated . . . visits   (D) fitness . . . exercise

   3. _____

Name _____

How well do you remember the words you studied in Lessons 34 through 36? Take the following test covering the words from the last three lessons.

Part 1 Choose the Correct Meaning

Each question below includes a word in capital letters, followed by four words or phrases. Choose the word or phrase that is <u>closest</u> in meaning to the word in capital letters. Write the letter for your answer on the line provided.

Sample

| S. FINISH | (A) enjoy | (B) complete | S. _____ |
| | (C) destroy | (D) enlarge | |

| 1. TRAIT | (A) path | (B) feature | 1. _____ |
| | (C) calmness | (D) buying and selling | |

| 2. STENCH | (A) foul smell | (B) long, narrow ditch | 2. _____ |
| | (C) strict rule | (D) type of tool | |

| 3. CONFISCATE | (A) confess | (B) remember | 3. _____ |
| | (C) take by force | (D) expand | |

| 4. TART | (A) legal action | (B) sour | 4. _____ |
| | (C) sweet | (D) sticky substance | |

| 5. INNOVATIVE | (A) youthful | (B) protected from disease | 5. _____ |
| | (C) original | (D) distasteful | |

| 6. COMMINGLE | (A) complicate | (B) confuse | 6. _____ |
| | (C) choose carefully | (D) combine | |

| 7. SAVOR | (A) rescue | (B) pursue | 7. _____ |
| | (C) accuse | (D) enjoy | |

| 8. BREED | (A) kind | (B) mental condition | 8. _____ |
| | (C) valuable possession | (D) brief statement | |

| 9. PERSISTENT | (A) partially hidden | (B) stubborn | 9. _____ |
| | (C) annoying | (D) meaningless | |

| 10. CONFIDE | (A) mislead | (B) express one's sorrow | 10. _____ |
| | (C) reveal | (D) gossip | |

11. DELECTABLE   (A) fresh   (B) foreign   11. _____
                  (C) delicious   (D) open

12. REAP   (A) understand   (B) plant   12. _____
                  (C) explain   (D) receive

13. PUNGENT   (A) easily angered   (B) sharp   13. _____
                  (C) rounded   (D) unsupported

14. COLLATE   (A) strain   (B) agree   14. _____
                  (C) place in order   (D) calculate

15. DISTINCTIVE   (A) unlike others   (B) twisted   15. _____
                  (C) worried   (D) broken into parts

Part 2 Matching Words and Meanings

Match the definition in Column B with the word in Column A. Write the letter of the correct definition on the line provided.

Column A	**Column B**	
16. collaborate	a. agreement	16. _____
17. reek	b. stink	17. _____
18. expertise	c. brief odor	18. _____
19. compromise	d. expression of sorrow	19. _____
20. whiff	e. special knowledge	20. _____
21. strive	f. attempt	21. _____
22. conformity	g. work together	22. _____
23. inquisitive	h. tempting	23. _____
24. appetizing	i. meet halfway	24. _____
25. condolence	j. curious	25. _____

Dictionary

Pronunciation Guide

Symbol	Example	Symbol	Example
ă	pat	oi	boy
ā	pay	ou	out
âr	care	o͝o	took
ä	father	o͞o	boot
ĕ	pet	ŭ	cut
ē	be	ûr	urge
ĭ	pit	th	thin
ī	pie	*th*	this
îr	pier	hw	which
ŏ	pot	zh	vision
ō	toe	ə	about, item
ô	paw		

Stress Marks: ′(primary); ′(secondary), as in **dictionary** (dĭk′shə-nĕr′ē)

A

ac·cess (ăk′ sĕs) *n.* **1.** The right, permission, or ability to approach, enter, or use: *Only qualified people have access to school records.* **2.** A way of approach: *The only access to the basement is through the kitchen.*

ac·quit (ə kwĭt′) *v.* **ac·quit·ted, ac·quit·ting, ac·quits.** To declare not guilty of a charge of crime or other offense: *The jury acquitted the woman of the charge of armed robbery.* — **ac·quit′tal** *n.*

a·dapt (ə dăpt′) *v.* **1.** To change or modify to meet new purposes: *We adapted the lawnmower engine to work in the go-cart.* **2.** To adjust to new circumstances: *It may take time to adapt to a new school.*

a·dept (ə dĕpt′) *adj.* Highly skilled: *The music teacher is an adept musician.* —**a·dept′ly** *adv.* — **a·dept′ness** *n.*

ad·min·is·tra·tion (ăd mĭn′ĭ strā′shən) *n.* **1.** The group of people who manage or direct an organization: *The school administration held a meeting with the parents of middle school students.* **2. the Administration.** The executive branch of the government, especially the President of the United States, the cabinet, and other officials.

a·dopt (ə dŏpt′) *v.* To take and use as one's own: *After living in Japan a short while, Sonia began to adopt some of the country's customs.*

ad·u·la·tion (ăj′ə lā′shən) *n.* Great praise to the point of being excessive: *The hometown team can count on the adulation of its fans.*

à la carte (ä′lə kärt′ *or* ăl′ə kärt′) *adv & adj.* With a separate price for each item on the menu: *The restaurant served all its food à la carte.*

al·lo·cate (ăl′ə kāt′) *v.* **al·lo·cat·ed, al·lo·cat·ing, al·lo·cates.** To set aside for a specific purpose: *The school district allocated money for new band uniforms.* —**al′lo·ca′tion** *n.*

al·lu·sion (ə lo͞o′zhən) *n.* An indirect or casual reference: *The television show contained an allusion to a famous novel.*

am·a·teur (ăm′ə tûr′ *or* ăm′ə cho͞or′ *or* ăm′ə tyo͞or′) *n.* **1.** A person who does something for pleasure rather than for money or as a profession: *The musicians in the community orchestra are amateurs.* **2.** A person who does something rather unskillfully: *The uneven hem looked as if it had been sewn by an amateur.* —*adj.* **1.** Relating to or done by amateurs. **2.** Not skillful.

am·ble (ăm′bəl) *v.* **am·bled, am·bling, am·bles.** To walk at a slow, relaxed, and leisurely pace: *The couple ambled through the park.* —**am′bler** *n.*

an·ces·tor (ăn′sĕs′tər) *n.* A person from whom one is descended: *Many people keep letters written by their ancestors.*

an·thol·o·gy (ăn thŏl′ə jē) *n., pl.* **an·thol·o·gies.** A collection of written work, often by different authors: *The anthology we use in English class contains short stories, poems, and plays.*

ap·pe·tiz·ing (ăp′ĭ tī′zĭng) *adj.* Arousing or creating a desire for food: *The chef arranged the food on the plate in an appetizing manner.* — **ap′pe·tiz′ing·ly** *adv.*

ap·pre·hen·sive (ăp′rĭ **hĕn**′sĭv) *adj.* Uneasy; afraid; anxious: *The girl was apprehensive about giving the speech in class.* —**ap′pre·hen′sive·ly** *adv.* —**ap′pre·hen′sive·ness** *n.*

ar·du·ous (är′jo͞o əs) *adj.* Requiring great effort; difficult to do: *Climbing to the top of the mountain was arduous.* —**ar′du·ous·ly** *adv.* —**ar′du·ous·ness** *n.*

a·ro·ma (ə rō′mə) *n., pl.* **a·ro·mas.** A pleasant smell or odor: *The aroma of popcorn filled the theater.*

ar·ray (ə rā′) *n.* **1.** A large, impressive group or collection: *The array of fall colors was breathtaking.* **2.** An orderly arrangement, especially of troups. **3.** Fine clothing. —*v.* **1.** To put in order. **2.** To dress up; adorn. —**ar·ray′er** *n.*

ar·ti·san (är′tĭ zən) *n.* A person skilled in a certain craft: *The artisan's beautiful vases were on display at the art gallery.*

as·cent (ə sĕnt′) *n.* **1.** Movement upward: *Our ascent up the steep cliff was slow.* **2.** An upward slope: *The car's engine stalled on the steep ascent of the mountain road.*

as·so·ci·ate (ə sō′shē ĭt *or* ə sō′sē ĭt) *n.* **1.** A coworker: *The lawyer and her associates meet every Monday to plan the week's work.* **2.** Friend; companion: *My associates and I enjoy going to the movies.*

as·sume (ə so͞om′) *v.* **as·sumed, as·sum·ing, as·sumes. 1.** Take on (the appearance, role of): *On Halloween the child assumed the appearance of a pumpkin.* **2.** To take for granted; suppose: *The teacher assumed that all of the students had read the story.* **3.** To take upon oneself: *When my mother is late, I assume the job of cooking dinner.* —**as·sum′a·ble** *adj.* —**as·sum′a·bly** *adv.* **as·sum′er** *n.*

at·tri·bute (ăt′rə byo͞ot′) *n.* A quality or characteristic of a person or thing: *One of the girl's attributes is courage.* —*v.* (ə trĭb′yo͞ot) **at·trib·ut·ed, at·trib·ut·ing, at·trib·utes.** To think of as belonging to or resulting from someone or something: *The success of the school is attributed to the principal.* —**at·trib′ut·a·ble** *adj.* —**at·trib′u·tor** *n.* —**at′tri·bu′tion** *n.*

B

ba·nal (bə năl′ *or* bā′nəl *or* bə näl′) *adj.* Dull or boring because of commonplace or overused expressions; *I started to daydream during the banal speech.* —**ba·nal′ly** *adv.*

ban·ish (băn′ĭsh) *v.* **1.** To force to leave: *The king banished his enemies to a foreign country.* **2.** To drive away: *I banished my fear of snakes by reading about them.*

bar·ba·rous (bär′bər əs) *adj.* **1.** Savage; uncivilized: *The barbarous people did not care about education.* **2.** Brutally cruel: *The people were shocked by the barbarous treatment of the prisoners of war.* —**bar′ba·rous·ly** *adv.*

bar·ren (băr′ən) *adj.* **1.** Unproductive; having little or no plant life: *In order to keep their fields from becoming barren, farmers rotate their crops.* **2.** Not able to bear offspring. **3.** Boring; uninteresting; empty: *For years the old man lived a barren life.* —**bar′ren·ness** *n.*

bar·ter (bär′tər) *v.* To trade or exchange goods or services without using money: *Every Saturday my friends and I barter our baseball cards.*

be·fall (bĭ fôl′) *v.* **be·fell** (bĭ fĕl′), **be·fall·en** (bĭ fô′lən), **be·fall·ing, be·falls.** To happen to; occur: *Columbus did not know what would befall him during his voyage in 1492.*

be·reaved (bĭ rēvd′) *adj.* Suffering the loss of a loved one: *The bereaved family was comforted by their friends.* —*n.* One who is or those who are bereaved: *The bereaved attended the funeral of their friend.*

be·stir (bĭ stûr′) *v.* **be·stirred, be·stir·ring, be·stirs.** To stir or provoke to action: *After the heavy snowstorm we bestirred ourselves to shovel the walks.*

be·stow (bĭ stō′) *v.* **be·stowed, be·stow·ing, be·stows.** To present, give, or grant as a gift or honor: *The mayor bestowed keys to the city on all the volunteers who had completed 500 hours of community service.*

bois·ter·ous (boi′stər əs *or* boi′strəs) *adj.* Noisy and lively; rowdy: *The boisterous fans celebrated the team's victory.* —**bois′ter·ous·ly** *adv.* —**bois′ter·ous·ness** *n.*

bon voy·age (bŏn′voi äzh′) *interj.* An expression used to wish a person a pleasant trip: *When I left for Europe, my friends wished me bon voyage.*

breed (brēd) *n.* **1.** A group or species of plants or animals having common ancestors and characteristics: *Certain breeds of dogs are more active than others.* **2.** A type, sort, or kind: *A serious breed of athlete trains for hours.* —*v.* To produce or cause to be.

brut·ish (bro͞o′tĭsh) *adj.* Like or resembling an animal or beast; stupid, coarse, savage, or cruel: *The man's brutish behavior embarrassed everyone in the room.* —**brut′ish·ly** *adv.* —**brut′ish·ness** *n.*

C

ca·pa·ble (kā′pə bəl) *adj.* Having ability; able: *Shana is a capable babysitter.* —**ca′pa·bly** *adv.*

cen·ten·a·ry (sĕn **tĕn′**ə rē *or* **sĕn′**tə nĕr′ē) *n., pl.*
cen·ten·a·ries. 1. A hundred years: *Technology
has become very important during the centenary
following 1900.* **2.** A hundredth anniversary or
celebration. —*adj.* Of or relating to a period of
one hundred years or a hundredth anniversary.

cin·e·ma·tog·ra·pher (sĭn′ə mə **tŏg′**rə fər) *n.* A motion picture photographer: *The cinematographer
won an Academy Award for the movie's beautiful
filming.*

cite (sīt) *v.* **cit·ed, cit·ing, cites.** To quote or mention as proof or support: *The parents cited several
instances when their children did outstanding
work.*

clam·or (**klăm′**ər) *n.* **1.** A loud, noisy, or strong
demand, complaint, or protest: *Many parents
took part in the clamor for crossing guards at the
school.* **2.** A loud, continuous uproar, as from a
crowd: *The clamor from the celebration lasted for
hours.* —*v.* To make loud, continuous noise.

cli·ent (**klī′**ənt) *n.* **1.** A person, group, or company
that uses the professional services of another,
such as an attorney: *The attorneys discussed the
case with their client.* **2.** A customer: *Successful
salespeople contact all of their clients at least
once a year.*

coax (kōks) *v.* To urge or persuade with soft, gentle
words, flattery, or manner: *We coaxed our friend
to ride the roller coaster with us.* —**coax′er** *n.*

co·ex·ist (kō′ĭg **zĭst′**) *v.* To live together at the same
time or in the same place: *Many kinds of animals
coexist in the forest.* —**co′ex·is′tence** *n.*
—**co′ex·is′tent** *adj.*

col·lab·o·rate (kə **lăb′**ə rāt′) *v.* **col·lab·o·rat·ed,
col·lab·o·rat·ing, col·lab·o·rates. 1.** To work
with another or others on a project: *The students
collaborated on the science project.* **2.** To help or
go along with an enemy that has invaded one's
country. —**col·lab′o·ra′tion** *n.*
—**col·lab′o·ra′tor** *n.*

col·late (kə **lāt′** *or* **kŏl′**āt′ *or* **kō′**lāt′) *v.* **col·lat·ed,
col·lat·ing, col·lates. 1.** To gather and put in
proper order: *The teacher collated the pages of the
test.* **2.** To examine and compare carefully and
critically: *The rare book dealer collated the two
very old books.*

com·mem·o·rate (kə **mĕm′**ə rāt′) *v.*
**com·mem·o·rat·ed, com·mem·o·rat·ing,
com·mem·o·rates. 1.** To honor the memory of:
*The school assembly commemorated the signing
of the Declaration of Independence.* **2.** To serve as
a memorial to: *The Vietnam Veterans Memorial
commemorates those Americans who died in the
Vietnam War.* —**com·mem′o·ra′tion** *n.*

com·merce (**kŏm′**ərs) *n.* The buying and selling
of goods and services, especially on a large scale:
Commerce was strong in some ancient civilizations.

com·min·gle (kə **mĭng′**gəl) *v.* **com·min·gled,
com·min·gling, com·min·gles.** To mix or blend
together; mingle: *The flavors of the herbs commin-
gled in the salad dressing.*

com·mon·place (**kŏm′**ən plās′) *adj.* Ordinary; uninteresting: *The new televison show was canceled
because it was so commonplace.*

com·pen·sa·tion (kŏm′pən **sā′**shən) *n.* Something
given as payment for work done, an injury, or a
loss; salary: *The workers involved in the accident
will receive compensation for their injuries.*

com·ple·ment (**kŏm′**plə mənt) *n.* Something that
completes or makes whole: *A glass of milk is a
nice complement to chocolate chip cookies.*

com·pli·ment (**kŏm′**plə mənt) *n.* An expression
of praise or admiration: *The singer received many
compliments after the concert.* —*v.* To give praise;
congratulate: *The teacher complimented her work.*

com·pro·mise (**kŏm′**prə mīz′) *n.* The settlement
of an argument, disagreement, or differences, by
having each side give up some of its claims or
demands and agree to some demands of the other:
*The treaty was signed because each country agreed
to the compromise.* —*v.* **com·pro·mised,
com·pro·mis·ing, com·pro·mis·es.** To make
a settlement by each side giving up some of its
claims or demands and agreeing to some demands of the other side.

con·cede (kən **sēd′**) *v.* **con·ced·ed, con·ced·ing,
con·cedes.** To admit as true: *After a long discussion the girl conceded that her friend's suggestion
was worth considering.*

con·clave (**kŏn′**klāv′) *n.* A private or secret gathering
or meeting: *Everyone who was invited attended the
conclave.*

con·cur (kən **kûr′**) *v.* **con·curred, con·cur·ring,
con·curs. 1.** To agree (with): *The family concurred
on where to go on vacation.* **2.** To happen at the
same time: *When cold weather and rain concur, it
is very unpleasant.*

con·do·lence (kən **dō′**ləns) *n.* An expression of
sympathy for someone who has suffered the loss
of a loved one or some other misfortune: *Many
people expressed their condolences at my grandfather's funeral.*

con·fer (kən **fûr′**) *v.* **con·ferred, con·fer·ring,
con·fers. 1.** To give as a gift or honor; to award:
The king conferred the title of knight upon the man.
2. To meet and discuss together: *The football players and coaches conferred about the next play.*

con·fide (kən **fīd**') *v.* **con·fid·ed, con·fid·ing, con·fides.** To tell privately and secretly: *The two best friends confide their secrets to each other.*

con·fis·cate (**kŏn**'fĭ skāt') *v.* **con·fis·cat·ed, con·fis·cat·ing, con·fis·cates.** To seize or take away by authority: *The police confiscated the illegal drugs.* —**con**'**fis·ca**'**tion** *n.*

con·form·i·ty (kən **fûr**'mĭ tē) *n., pl.* **con·form·i·ties. 1.** Behavior, action, or thought in agreement with current customs, rules, standards, or styles: *Students' conformity with the school rules is expected.* **2.** Similarity; agreement: *The teacher insisted that we speak in conformity with standard English.*

con·se·quence (**kŏn**'sĭ kwĕns') *n.* A result of an earlier happening or action; outcome: *The consequence of not studying for the test was a failing grade.*

con·ser·va·to·ry (kən **sûr**'və tôr'e) *n., pl.* **con·ser·va·to·ries.** A school of music, dramatic art, or other arts: *Music students from the conservatory gave a recital.*

con·sis·ten·cy (kən **sĭs**'tən sē) *n., pl.* **con·sis·ten·cies. 1.** A keeping to a way of thinking or acting: *The boss could count on the secretary's consistency.* **2.** Degree of firmness, thickness, or density: *The consistency of the milkshake was like water.* **3.** Agreement or harmony among things or parts: *There is no consistency between the witnesses' accounts of the accident.*

con·so·la·tion (kŏn'sə **lā**'shən) *n.* Something that comforts: *Our consolation for losing the game was that we lost by only one point during overtime.*

con·spire (kən **spīr**') *v.* **con·spired, con·spir·ing, con·spires.** To plan together secretly: *The two thieves conspired to rob the bank.*

con·sult·ant (kən **sŭl**'tənt) *n.* A person who gives expert, professional, or technical advice: *The store owner asked a tax consultant for advice.*

con·tem·plate (**kŏn**'təm plāt') *v.* **con·tem·plat·ed, con·tem·plat·ing, con·tem·plates.** To think about or look at carefully: *The mathematician contemplated the problem for a week before suggesting a solution.*

con·vene (kən **vēn**') *v.* **con·vened, con·ven·ing, con·venes.** To come together or cause to come together, especially for a meeting: *The president of the student council convened a meeting.*

con·ven·ience (kən **vēn**'yəns) *n.* **1.** The quality of being easy to do or use, or handy: *Sometimes we take the convenience of computers for granted.* **2.** Anything that gives comfort or saves work: *The microwave oven is a convenience that speeds meal preparation.*

con·vert (kən **vûrt**') *v.* **1.** To change in character, form, condition, or use: *In the summer the iceskating rink is converted to a rollerblading rink.* **2.** To cause to change to a different belief, religion, or action: *The candidate converted most of the voters to his ideas.*

con·vey (kən **vā**') *v.* To take, move, or carry from one place to another: *The traders conveyed goods to the trading post.*

cor·pu·lent (**kôr**'pyə lənt) *adj.* Fat; overweight: *The corpulent dog could barely walk.* —**cor**'**pu·lence** *n.*

cow·er (**kou**'ər) *v.* To crouch, cringe, or shrink away, as from fear, pain, or shame: *Because a dog was chasing it, the fox cowered in a hollow tree.*

cur·ric·u·lum (kə **rĭk**'yə ləm) *n., pl.* **cur·ric·u·la** (kə **rĭk**'yə lə) or **cur·ric·u·lums.** A course of study offered at a school or department: *The English curriculum included a grammar course.*

D

de·cath·lon (dĭ **kăth**'lən *or* dĭ **kăth**'lŏn') *n.* A track and field contest made up of ten events: *The decathlon is a popular event in the Olympics.*

de·ceased (dĭ **sēst**') *adj.* Dead: *They built a monument to honor the deceased mayor.*

de·coy (**dē**'koi' *or* dĭ **koi**') *n.* **1.** A person or thing used to lure another into danger or a trap: *The wallet was used as a decoy to catch the pickpocket.* **2.** A model of a duck or other bird used to lure other birds within gun range. —*v.* To lure into a trap or danger by a trick.

de·face (dĭ **fās**') *v.* **de·faced, de·fac·ing, de·fac·es.** To spoil or mar the appearance of: *Vandals defaced the statue in the park.* —**de·face**'**ment** *n.*

de·fect (**dē**'fĕkt' *or* dĭ **fĕkt**') *n.* **1.** A flaw; blemish; imperfection: *The defect in the computer was easily repaired.* —*v.* (di fekt'). To abandon a cause, country, or group, especially to go to a group opposing it. —**de·fec**'**tion** *n.* —**de·fec**'**tor** *n.*

de·fec·tive (dĭ **fĕk**'tĭv) *adj.* Having flaws or imperfections; imperfect: *The speakers on my new radio were defective, so I exchanged it.*

de·fer (dĭ **fûr**') *v.* **de·ferred, de·fer·ring, de·fers.** To put off; postpone: *We will defer the picnic until spring.* —**de·fer**'**ra·ble** *adj.*

de·fi·cient (dĭ **fĭsh**'ənt) *adj.* Lacking something that is necessary or essential; insufficient: *My exercise program is deficient in aerobic activities.*

de·for·mi·ty (dĭ **fôr**'mĭ tē) *n., pl.* **de·for·mi·ties.** A condition of being improperly formed: *Biologists studied the five-legged frogs to find the cause of the deformities.*

de·grade (dĭ grād′) v. **de·grad·ed, de·grad·ing, de·grades.** To lower in quality, character, or dignity; dishonor: *Sloppiness and uncleanliness degrade a person.*

de·hy·drate (dē hī′drāt′) v. **de·hy·drat·ed, de·hy·drat·ing, de·hy·drates.** To remove or lose water or moisture from; dry: *Juan had to drink a lot of water because his high temperature dehydrated him.*

de·lec·ta·ble (dĭ lĕk′tə bəl) adj. Very delicious or delightful: *The juicy peach was delectable.*

del·e·gate (dĕl′ĭ gāt′) v. **del·e·gat·ed, del·e·gat·ing, del·e·gates.** To give or assign (responsibility, power, or authority) to another: *Every week the teacher delegated the duty of being crossing guards to two students.* —n. (dĕl′ĭ gāt′ or dĕl′ĭ gĭt) n. A person chosen to act for or represent another: *The president of the organization is a delegate to the national convention.*

de·lib·er·ate (dĭ lĭb′ə rāt′) v. **de·lib·er·at·ed, de·lib·er·at·ing, de·lib·er·ates.** To think or consider carefully: *The jury deliberated for two days before reaching a decision.* —adj. (dĭ lĭb′ər ĭt) adj. Carefully thought out; intentional: *Tracy's lie was a deliberate attempt to get me into trouble.* —**de·lib′er·ate·ly** adv. —**de·lib′er·ate·ness** n.

del·i·cate (dĕl′ĭ kĭt) adj. **1.** Fine in quality, structure, texture, or form: *The dishes were made of delicate china.* **2.** Pleasing to the senses in a mild way: *The color of the sky was a delicate blue.* **3.** Easily broken: *I was afraid I would break the delicate glass.* —**del′i·cate·ly** adv. —**del′i·cate·ness** n.

del·i·ca·tes·sen (dĕl′ĭ kə tĕs′ən) n. A store that sells prepared foods such as cheese, cooked meats, and salads: *We got sandwiches at the delicatessen.*

de·nounce (dĭ nouns′) v. **de·nounced, de·nounc·ing, de·nounc·es. 1.** To speak against publicly: *The candidate denounced her opponent's position on taxes.* **2.** To accuse: *The nosy neighbor denounced the children to their parents.*

de·pend·en·cy (dĭ pĕn′dən sē) n., pl. **de·pend·en·cies.** The state of relying on someone or something for aid or support: *The dependency of children on their parents often lasts until the children are adults.*

de·plete (dĭ plēt′) v. **de·plet·ed, de·plet·ing, de·pletes.** To use up; decrease the amount of: *The pioneers had to be careful not to deplete their supplies during the winter.* —**de·ple′tion** n.

de·prive (dĭ prīv′) v. **de·prived, de·priv·ing, de·prives. 1.** To take away: *The prison sentence deprived the criminal of the right to vote.* **2.** To keep from having: *Camping in the wilderness deprives one of many modern conveniences.*

de·scend (dĭ sĕnd′) v. **1.** To go or come down to a lower place: *The mountain goat was able to descend quickly from the top of the cliff.* **2.** To slope downward: *The road descended down and around a long hill.*

de·tain (dĭ tān′) v. **1.** To keep from leaving; to keep in custody: *The FBI detained the suspected kidnapper.* **2.** To delay: *My friends detained me for more than an hour.* —**de·tain′ment** n.

de·ten·tion (dĭ tĕn′shən) n. The act of holding back or state of being held back; confinement: *The suspect is in detention until the trial.*

de·te·ri·o·rate (dĭ tîr′ē ə rāt′) v. **de·te·ri·o·rat·ed, de·te·ri·o·rat·ing, de·te·ri·o·rates.** To lessen or become worse in quality, character, condition, or value: *The paint on the house began to deteriorate after fifteen years.* —**de·te′ri·o·ra′tion** n.

de·ter·rent (dĭ tûr′ənt or dĭ tŭr′ənt) n. Something that prevents or discourages someone from doing something, especially from fear or doubt: *Fear of heights is a deterrent to climbing mountains.* —adj. Tending to discourage or keep from doing something.

de·void (dĭ void′) adj. Completely without; empty: *The movie was devoid of any excitement.*

di·a·logue (dī′ə lôg′ or dī′ə lŏg′) n. **1.** Conversation between two or more people: *The dialogue between the two friends was witty.* **2.** The conversation between characters in a play, movie, or book: *Some authors have difficulty making their characters' dialogue sound realistic.*

dis·arm (dĭs ärm′) v. **1.** To take away a weapon or weapons from: *The police disarmed the suspected murderer.* **2.** To make harmless: *When at last the expert was able to disarm the bomb, everyone was relieved.*

dis·ar·ray (dĭs′ə rā′) n. A state of disorder or confusion: *Because my closet was in such disarray I couldn't find my shoes.* —v. To throw into disorder or confusion.

dis·a·vow (dĭs ə vou′) v. To deny knowledge of, responsibility for, or association with: *The candidate disavowed having taken campaign funds illegally.*

dis·claim (dĭs klām′) v. To give up or deny any claim to, responsibility for, or connection with: *Marcus disclaimed any knowledge of the broken window.*

dis·close (dĭ sklōz′) v. **dis·closed, dis·clos·ing, dis·clos·es. 1.** To make known; reveal: *The judge disclosed his decision by posting it on the Internet.* **2.** To uncover: *Digging disclosed a time capsule buried years before.*

dis·cred·it (dĭs **krĕd′**ĭt) *v.* **1.** To cast doubt or disbelief on: *The investigation discredited the woman's story.* **2.** To disgrace: *Misbehavior on field trips discredits the whole class.* —*n.* Doubt. *The people's discredit of the tax proposal was because of questionable past actions.*

dis·en·gage (dĭs′ĕn **gāj′**) *v.* **dis·en·gaged, dis·en·gag·ing, dis·en·gag·es. 1.** To release or loosen something that holds, entangles, or connects: *The farmer disengaged the animal caught in the fence.* **2.** To free oneself from an obligation, engagement, or promise: *Busy students sometimes need to disengage themselves from some activities.* —**dis′en·gage′ment** *n.*

di·shev·eled (dĭ **shĕv′**əld) *adj.* Not neat; untidy; disorderly: *Her disheveled hair was the result of strong winds.*

dis·il·lu·sion (dĭs′ĭ **loo′**zhən) *v.* To free from a false belief or idea: *Actors sometimes become disillusioned about the glamorous life of a star.* —**dis′il·lu′sion·ment** *n.*

dis·pu·tant (dĭ **spyoot′**nt *or* **dĭs′**pyə tənt) *n.* A person who is involved in an argument or debate: *A week after the argument the disputants met to settle their differences.*

dis·tinc·tive (dĭ **stĭngk′**tĭv) *adj.* Serving to set apart from others or identify; characteristic: *Curiosity is a distinctive quality of cats.* —**dis·tinc′tive·ly** *adv.* —**dis·tinc′tive·ness** *n.*

dis·tort (dĭ **stôrt′**) *v.* **1.** To twist the truth; misrepresent: *The scientist said the newspaper article distorted the facts about global warming.* **2.** To twist or bend something out of shape: *Some comedians can distort their faces and mimic the voices of others.*

di·ver·sion (dĭ **vûr′**zhən *or* dī **vûr′**zhən) *n.* **1.** Something that draws the mind or attention in another direction: *One parent may create a diversion while the other lights the candles on the birthday cake.* **2.** Something that entertains: *Music is a favorite diversion of mine.*

di·ver·si·ty (dĭ **vûr′**sĭ tē *or* dī **vûr′**sĭ tē) *n., pl.* **di·ver·si·ties. 1.** Difference: *The diversity of the members of our class helps us to learn about different cultures.* **2.** Variety: *Our discussions are interesting because of the diversity of opinions that we hold.*

doubt (dout) *v.* **1.** To be uncertain or unconvinced about: *The girl doubted the answer to her question.* **2.** To be uncertain of; distrust: *I shouldn't doubt my friend's honesty.* **3.** To think of as unlikely: *The coach doubted that the team could win the match.*

draft (drăft) *n.* The first or early version of a piece of writing: *The teacher corrects the first draft of our essays but doesn't give us a grade on it.*

du·bi·ous (**doo′**bē əs *or* **dyoo′**bē əs) *adj.* **1.** Feeling or showing uncertainty; skeptical: *His friends were dubious that he could run the mile in four minutes.* **2.** Causing doubt: *The dubious explanation was confusing.* —**du′bi·ous·ly** *adv.*

E

ef·fec·tu·al (ĭ **fĕk′**choo əl) *adj.* Bringing about or able to bring about a desired effect; truly effective: *The coach's new plan was effectual in leading the team to a state championship.* —**ef·fec′tu·al·ly** *adv.* —**ef·fec′tu·al·ness** *n.*

e·lab·o·rate (ĭ **lăb′**ər it) *adj.* Planned or worked out in great detail; complicated: *The elaborate plans for the wedding were very time consuming.* —*v.* (ĭ **lăb′**ə rāt′). **e·lab·o·rat·ed, e·lab·o·rat·ing, e·lab·o·rates. 1.** To plan or work out in great detail. **2.** To add more details. —**e·lab′o·rate·ly** *adv.* —**e·lab′o·rate·ness** *n.* —**e·lab′o·ra′tion** *n.*

em·bar·go (ĕm **bär′**gō) *n., pl.* **em·bar·goes.** A government restriction on trade with a foreign country, especially import, export, or sale of certain items: *The embargo against the country did not include medical supplies.*

em·brace (ĕm **brās′**) *v.* **em·braced, em·brac·ing, em·brac·es.** To take up willingly; eagerly engage in: *The young skater embraced the sport of hockey.*

en·cir·cle (ĕn **sûr′**kəl) *v.* **en·cir·cled, en·cir·cling, en·cir·cles.** To form a circle around; surround: *The shade garden encircles the tree.*

en·dorse (ĕn **dôrs′**) *v.* **en·dorsed, en·dors·ing, en·dors·es. 1.** To support or approve: *The principal agreed to endorse the plan for the new theater.* **2.** To sign one's name on the back of a check or similar document: *Remember to endorse the check before you deposit it.* —**en·dors′er** *n.*

en·ter·prise (**en′**tər prīz′) *n.* A project or undertaking, especially one that is important, difficult, or risky: *The sale of personal computers is a successful business enterprise.*

en·tomb (ĕn **toom′**) *v.* To place in a tomb, grave, or chamber; bury: *When the woman died, she was entombed in the family burial chamber.* —**en·tomb′ment** *n.*

ep·ic (**ĕp′**ĭk) *n.* **1.** A long poem about the adventures and deeds of a legendary super hero: *The Odyssey is an epic about the Greek hero Odysseus.* **2.** A written work that has the qualities of an epic. —**ep′i·cal·ly** *adv.*

ep·i·gram (ĕp′ĭ grăm′) *n.* A short, witty statement or poem: *The clever author was famous for his epigrams.*

e·qua·tor (ĭ kwā′tər) *n.* An imaginary line around the center of the earth that is halfway between the North and South Poles.

e·ra (îr′ə *or* ĕr′ə) *n.* **1.** A period of time marked by certain or special events, ideas, or persons: *Many people moved from farms to cities during the industrial era.* **2.** A period of time measured from some important event: *The launching of Sputnik was the beginning of the space era.* **3.** A major division of geologic time, such as an Ice Age.

es·ti·mate (ĕs′tə māt′) *v.* **es·ti·mat·ed, es·ti·mat·ing, es·ti·mates.** To form a judgment of opinion about the cost, quantity, size, or extent of something; guess: *The police estimated the size of the crowd.* —*n.* (ĕs′tə mit) A rough guess. *My estimate is that I will finish my homework in an hour.*

ex·ceed (ĭk sēd′) *v.* **1.** To be greater than; surpass: *The attendance at the game exceeded our expectations.* **2.** To go beyond the limits of: *The driver got a ticket for exceeding the speed limit.*

ex·ces·sive (ĭk sĕs′iv) *adj.* More than necessary, reasonable, or usual; too much: *The passenger's outburst over the slight delay seemed excessive.* —**ex·ces′sive·ly** *adv.* —**ex·ces′sive·ness** *n.*

ex·em·pla·ry (ĭg zĕm′plə rē) *adv.* Worthy of being a model or example: *Juan received an award for his exemplary attendance because he did not miss any classes all year.* —**ex·em′pla·ri·ly** *adv.*

ex·hume (ĭg zōōm′ *or* ĭg zyōōm′) *v.* **ex·humed, ex·hum·ing, ex·humes.** To dig up or remove from the earth or a grave: *The body was exhumed so it could be buried in a family cemetery.*

ex·pe·di·tion (ĕk′spĭ dĭsh′ən) *n.* **1.** A trip made for a specific purpose: *Lewis and Clark's expedition up the Missouri River provided valuable information about the frontier.* **2.** The people and equipment that make such a trip.

ex·per·tise (ĕk spûr tēz′) *n.* Special skill or knowledge: *The operation was a success because of the surgeon's expertise.*

ex·pul·sion (ĭk spŭl′shən) *n.* The act of forcing or driving out or the state of being forced to leave or driven out: *The punishment for the most serious behavior problems is expulsion from school.*

ex·qui·site (ĕk′skwĭ zĭt *or* ĭk skwĭz′ĭt) *adj.* Very beautiful, delicate, or charming: *Her exquisite necklace was made of diamonds and pearls.* —**ex′qui·site·ly** *adv.*

ex·traor·di·nar·y (ĭk strôr′dn ĕr′ē *or* ĕk strə ôr′dn ĕr′ē) *adj.* Beyond what is usual or expected; remarkable: *It is extraordinary to hit sixty home runs in one baseball season.* —**ex·traor′di·nar′i·ly** *adv.*

ex·trav·a·gance (ĭk străv′ə gəns) *n.* **1.** Wasteful or excessive spending of money: *The woman's extravagance caused her bank account to be overdrawn.* **2.** Something that is too expensive: *The large television set was an extravagance for the family.*

ex·tro·vert (ĕk′strə vûrt′) *n.* An outgoing person whose interest is more with other people and events than with his or her own thoughts or feelings: *My friend is an extrovert who likes to meet new people.*

F

fa·ble (fā′bəl) *n.* A short story, usually featuring animals as characters, that teaches a lesson: *The teacher read a fable to her first-grade class.*

fa·cade (fə säd′) *n.* **1.** The front of a building: *The facade of the museum was made of marble.* **2.** A false front; illusion: *After his pass was intercepted, the quarterback's smile was a facade.*

fal·li·ble (făl′ə bəl) *adj.* Able to make mistakes or err: *The famous actor was proven to be fallible when he forgot his lines.* —**fal′li·bil′i·ty** *n.* —**fal′li·bly** *adv.*

fault (fôlt) *n.* **1.** A mistake; error: *The entire performance was without a fault.* **2.** Flaw: *The fault in the concrete caused the sidewalk to crumble.* **3.** Responsibility for a mistake or error: *The forest fire wasn't anybody's fault.*

feat (fēt) *n.* An outstanding deed, achievement, or act: *Launching a rocket ship into space is an amazing feat.*

fee·ble (fē′bəl) *adj.* **fee·bler, fee·blest.** **1.** Weak: *After her illness, the patient was feeble.* **2.** Without force, strength, power, or effectiveness: *I made a feeble attempt to learn to play the violin.* —**fee′ble·ness** *n.* —**fee′bly** *adv.*

fe·ro·cious (fə rō′shəs) *adj.* Extremely fierce; dangerous: *Some dinosaurs were ferocious animals.* —**fe·ro′cious·ly** *adv.* —**fe·ro′cious·ness** *n.*

flab·ber·gast (flăb′ər găst′) *v.* To overcome with surprise or amazement. *My sister's acting talent flabbergasts me.*

flab·ber·gast·ed (flăb′ər găst′əd) *adj.* Astonished; amazed: *Seth was flabbergasted when he won the sweepstakes.*

fore·shad·ow (fôr shăd′ō) *v.* To suggest or provide clues beforehand of what will happen later: *The author gave many hints that foreshadowed the sad ending.*

fore·thought (fôr′thôt′) *n.* Thought, care, or planning for the future: *Forethought is important when choosing a career.*

for·swear (fôr swâr′) *v.* **for·swore** (fôr swôr′), **for·sworn** (fôr swôrn′), **for·swear·ing, for·swears.** To give up or reject seriously: *After reading about skin cancer, I forswore lying in the sun without sunscreen.*

fra·grance (frā′grəns) *n.* A sweet or pleasant smell: *The fragrance of flowers filled the room.*

fraud·u·lent (frô′jə lənt) *adj.* **1.** Based on, using, or taking part in deceit or trickery; dishonest: *The people were tricked by the fraudulent sale of rare toys that were really worthless.* —**fraud′u·lence** *n.* —**fraud′u·lent·ly** *adv.*

frig·id (frĭj′ĭd) *adj.* **1.** Very cold: *When the furnace broke, the house became frigid.* **2.** Lacking warmth or friendliness: *After the argument the girls were frigid toward each other.* —**fri·gid′i·ty, frig′id·ness** *n.* —**frig′id·ly** *adv.*

friv·o·lous (frĭv′ə ləs) *adj.* Unimportant: *It seemed frivolous to worry about a small toy, when the tornado had destroyed the entire house.* —**friv′o·lous·ly** *adv.* —**friv′o·lous·ness** *n.*

G

gait (gāt) *n.* **1.** A way of walking, running, or stepping: *The old man's slow gait was caused by arthritis.* **2.** The way a horse moves.

gaud·y (gô′dē) *adj.* **gaud·i·er, gaud·i·est.** Tastelessly brightly colored or showy: *The gaudy dress was not appropriate for a job interview.* —**gaud′i·ly** *adv.* —**gaud′i·ness** *n.*

gild (gĭld) *v.* To coat with a thin layer of gold: *The artist gilded the statue.*

gild·ed (gĭld′əd) *adj.* Covered with a thin layer of gold: *The gilded ornament was worth a great deal of money.*

graph·ic (grăf′ĭk) *adj.* Vividly or clearly described: *Readers feel as though they are part of the story because of its graphic description of events.* —*n.* A picture, map, or computer-generated image: *We were amazed at the detail in the graphic drawn on the computer.* —**graph′i·cal·ly** *adv.*

H

har·ass (hăr′əs *or* hə răs′) *v.* **ha·rassed, ha·rass·ing, ha·rass·es.** To bother, annoy, or torment repeatedly: *The bully got into trouble for harassing the younger children.* —**ha·rass′ment** *n.*

hex·a·gon (hĕk′sə gŏn′) *n.* A plane figure with six angles and six sides: *The diamond in the engagement ring is in the shape of a hexagon.*

hi·lar·i·ous (hĭ lâr′ē əs *or* hĭ lăr′ē əs) *adj.* Very funny: *Everyone left the hilarious movie in a good mood.* —**hi·lar′i·ous·ly** *adv.*

I

il·lu·mi·na·tion (ĭ lōō′mə nā′shən) *n.* **1.** A source of light or brightness: *The flashlight was the only illumination the hikers had at night.* **2.** Decoration with light: *The illumination of the building was beautiful.*

il·lu·sion (ĭ lōō′zhən) *n.* An unreal, false, or misleading appearance: *The illusion of water can fool people traveling in the desert.*

im·ma·ture (ĭm′ə tyōōr′ *or* ĭm′ə tōōr′ *or* ĭm′ə chōōr′) *adj.* Not fully grown or developed; childish: *The immature dog still acted like a puppy.* —**im′ma·ture′ly** *adv.* —**im′ma·tur′i·ty** *n.*

im·mod·er·ate (ĭ mŏd′ər ĭt) *adj.* Going beyond normal or proper limits; excessive: *Celia got sick after eating an immoderate amount of candy.* —**im·mod′er·ate·ly** *adv.*

im·pec·ca·ble (ĭm pĕk′ə bəl) *adj.* Without error, defect, or fault; flawless: *The dancers gave an impeccable performance.* —**im·pec′ca·bly** *adv.*

im·pen·e·tra·ble (ĭm pĕn′ĭ trə bəl) *adj.* **1.** Impossible to pierce, enter, or pass through: *The walls of the building were impenetrable.* **2.** Impossible to understand: *That problem is impenetrable.* —**im·pen′e·tra·bly** *adv.*

im·per·ti·nence (ĭm pûr′tn əns) *n.* **1.** Rudeness; insolence: *The child's impertinence toward the teacher was unusual.* **2.** A rude act or remark: *The teenager was grounded for a week for the impertinence.*

im·prob·a·ble (ĭm prŏb′ə bəl) *adj.* Unlikely: *The jury did not believe the improbable story of the accused person.* —**im·prob′a·bil′i·ty** *n.* —**im·prob′a·bly** *adv.*

in·ac·ces·si·ble (ĭn′ăk sĕs′ə bəl) *adj.* Difficult to reach or approach: *The auditorium is inaccessible to people in wheelchairs.* —**in′ac·ces′si·bly** *adv.*

in·au·di·ble (ĭn ô′də bəl) *adj.* Impossible to hear: *Since there were no microphones, the speech was inaudible.* —**in·au′di·bly** *adv.*

in·co·her·ent (ĭn′kō hîr′ənt) *adj.* **1.** Not connected in a logical or meaningful way: *The letter was so poorly organized that it was incoherent.* **2.** Not able to express oneself in a clear or orderly way: *The driver was incoherent after the accident.* —**in′co·her′ence** *n.* —**in′co·her′ent·ly** *adv.*

in·com·pe·tent (ĭn kŏm′pĭ tənt) *adj.* Without enough ability, knowledge, or qualifications; not capable: *The new employee was incompetent and* could not do the job. —**in·com′pe·tence** *n.* —**in·com′pe·tent·ly** *adv.*

in·de·ci·sive (ĭn′dĭ **sī′**sĭv) *adj.* **1.** Not able to make up one's mind: *The store had so many toys that the children were indecisive about what they wanted.* —**in′de·ci′sive·ly** *adv.* —**in′de·ci′sive·ness** *n.*

in·dis·pen·sa·ble (ĭn′dĭ **spĕn′**sə bəl) *adj.* Absolutely necessary; essential: *A refrigerator is an indispensable appliance.*

in·fe·ri·or (ĭn **fîr′**ē ər) *adj.* **1.** Of poor quality: *The tire on my bicycle was inferior, so I had to replace it.* **2.** Low or lower in rank, value, or importance: *Because I had difficulty understanding math, I felt inferior to my classmates.*

in·fil·trate (ĭn **fĭl′**trāt *or* ĭn′fĭl trāt′) *v.* **in·fil·trat·ed, in·fil·trat·ing, in·fil·trates.** To filter into or through: *The fine sand infiltrated my mesh beach bag.* —**in′fil·tra′tion** *n.*

in·fla·tion (ĭn **flā′**shən) *n.* An increase in the price of goods and services: *Because of inflation gasoline costs more now than it did twenty years ago.*

in·fu·ri·ate (ĭn **fyoor′**ē āt′) *v.* **in·fu·ri·at·ed, in·fu·ri·at·ing, in·fu·ri·ates.** To make furious; enrage: *People who make fun of others infuriate me.*

in·fu·ri·at·ed (ĭn **fyoor′**ē āt′əd) *adj.* Enraged: *The infuriated teacher kept the class after school.*

in·ge·nu·i·ty (ĭn′jə **noo′**ĭ tē *or* ĭn′jə **nyoo′**ĭ tē) *n.*, *pl.* **in·ge·nu·i·ties.** The quality of having or showing cleverness, creativity, or imagination: *The pioneers had to have ingenuity in order to survive.*

in·no·va·tive (ĭn′ə vā′tĭv) *adj.* **1.** Able or tending to introduce new ideas: *The innovative movie director used stunning special effects in the film.* **2.** Characterized by being new: *Innovative laser surgery has changed how long patients stay in the hospital.*

in·nu·mer·a·ble (ĭ **noo′**mər ə bəl *or* ĭ **nyoo′**mər ə bəl) *adj.* Too many to be counted: *There were innumerable bees in the hive.*

in·quis·i·tive (ĭn **kwĭz′**ĭ tĭv) *adj.* Eager to find out information; curious: *Little children are inquisitive about their surroundings.* —**in·quis′i·tive·ly** *adv.* —**in·quis′i·tive·ness** *n.*

in·scribe (ĭn **skrīb′**) *v.* **in·scribed, in·scrib·ing, in·scribes.** **1.** To mark, write, print, carve, or engrave (words or characters) on a surface: *The sculptor inscribed his name on the sculpture.* **2.** To mark, write, print, carve, or engrave with words or characters: *The builder inscribed the cornerstone with the date the building was completed.*

in·ter·cede (ĭn′tər **sēd′**) *v.* **in·ter·ced·ed, in·ter·ced·ing, in·ter·cedes.** **1.** To come between two sides in an effort to settle an argument or dispute: *The teacher interceded in the argument between the two boys.* **2.** To plead on behalf of another: *My sister interceded with my mother to let me stay up later.*

in·trigue (ĭn **trēg′**) *v.* **1. in·trigued, in·trigu·ing, in·trigues.** To capture interest or curiosity; fascinate: *Space exploration has intrigued people for years.* **2.** To plot secretly. —*n.* (**ĭn′**trēg′). A secret plot.

in·tro·vert (**ĭn′**trə vûrt′) *n.* A person whose interest is more with his or her own thoughts and feelings rather than with other people and events around him or her: *An introvert is happiest being alone.*

in·tu·i·tion (ĭn′too **ĭsh′**ən *or* ĭn′tyoo **ĭsh′**ən) *n.* A sensing, knowing, or understanding of something not based on reasoning, facts, or proof: *My intuition told me that something was wrong even before I heard the news.*

in·ven·to·ry (**ĭn′**vən tôr′ē) *n.*, *pl.* **in·ven·to·ries.** **1.** All of the goods in stock available for selling: *The entire inventory of swimsuits was on sale.* **2.** A detailed list of all goods in stock. **3.** The act of making such a list. —*v.* **in·ven·to·ried, in·ven·to·ry·ing, in·ven·to·ries.** To make a detailed list of all the items in stock.

in·vert (ĭn **vûrt′**) *v.* **1.** To turn upside down: *I inverted my plate, and the food landed on the carpet.* **2.** To reverse the order, direction, position, or condition of: *I carelessly inverted the words in the title of my essay.*

in·ves·tor (ĭn **vĕst′**ər) *n.* A person who puts money into something, such as property, a business, or stocks, in order to make a profit: *The investors in the company receive an annual report that tells them how the company is doing.*

in·vo·ca·tion (ĭn′və **kā′**shən) *n.* An appeal for help, especially from a higher power: *The tribe gave an invocation for the return of the buffalo.*

in·voke (ĭn **vōk′**) *v.* **in·voked, in·vok·ing, in·vokes.** **1.** To ask for help or protection: *The citizens invoked the mayor to lower taxes.* **2.** To beg for sincerely: *The convicted robber invoked the judge for mercy.*

ir·re·vers·i·ble (ĭr′ĭ **vûr′**sə bəl) *adj.* Incapable of being changed; unchangeable; permanent: *Even though the umpire made a bad call, it was irreversible.* —**ir′re·vers′i·bly** *adv.*

J

jaunt (jônt *or* jänt) *n.* A short, pleasant trip: *Our weekend jaunt to the state park was enjoyable.*

L

lac·er·ate (lăs′ə rāt′) *v.* **lac·er·at·ed, lac·er·at·ing, lac·er·ates.** To tear or rip roughly, especially in an injury: *I accidentally lacerated my hand with a bread knife.*

lam·baste (lăm bāst′) *v.* **lam·bast·ed, lam·bast·ing, lam·bastes. 1.** To scold harshly: *The mother lambasted her daughter for being two hours late.* **2.** To beat or thrash soundly.

lo·cale (lō kăl′) *n.* A particular place, especially with reference to events or circumstances connected with it: *The locale of the new school is convenient for many students.*

loft·y (lôf′tē *or* lŏf′tē) *adj.* **loft·i·er, loft·i·est. 1.** Important, high, or elevated in dignity, rank, character, or spirit: *The explorers had lofty goals.* **2.** Very high; towering: *The lofty mountain peaks were covered with snow.* **—loft′i·ly** *adv.*

loi·ter (loi′tər) *v.* **1.** To stand around idly and aimlessly: *The teenagers loitered at the street corner.* **2.** To move slowly with frequent stops: *The shoppers loitered in the mall as they looked into the stores' windows.* **—loi′ter·er** *n.*

lu·mi·nous (lōō′mə nəs) *adj.* **1.** Giving off light; shining; bright: *The luminous comet could be seen for a month.* **2.** Easily understood; clear: *The luminous explanation helped us understand astronomy.* **—lu′mi·nous·ly** *adv.* **— lu′mi·nous·ness** *n.*

lurk (lûrk) *v.* **1.** To sneak about: *The thief lurked in the shadows of the building.* **2.** To lie hidden, ready to attack: *The cat lurked under the birdhouse.* **—lurk′er** *n.*

lus·trous (lŭs′trəs) *adj.* Shining: *The new car had a lustrous red finish.* **—lus′trous·ly** *adv.* **— lus′trous·ness** *n.*

M

maim (mām) *v.* To injure or disable severely; cripple: *The swimmer was maimed by a vicious shark.*

ma·neu·ver (mə nōō′vər *or* mə nyōō′vər) *n.* A skillful, clever, or cunning move or procedure; scheme: *The boy won the chess game because of a surprise maneuver.* **—***v.* To plan or perform skillfully: *The taxi driver was able to maneuver through the heavy traffic.* **—ma·neu′ver·a·bil′i·ty** *n.* **—ma·neu′ver·a·ble** *adj.*

mar·gin·al (mär′jə nəl) *adj.* **1.** Barely good enough: *Even though my violin playing is marginal, I am in the orchestra.* **2.** Making a very small profit: *The store went out of business because its profits were marginal.* **—mar′gin·al·ly** *adv.*

mau·so·le·um (mô′sə lē′əm *or* mô′zə lē′əm) *n., pl.* **mau·so·le·ums** *or* **mau·so·le·a.** A large, stately building housing a tomb: *Many kings and queens were buried in the mausoleum.*

mea·ger (mē′gər) *adj.* Barely enough in amount or quality; scanty: *The shipwrecked sailors had a meager supply of food and water.* **—mea′ger·ly** *adv.*— **mea′ger·ness** *n.*

me·di·o·cre (mē′dē ō′kər) *adj.* Neither good nor bad; ordinary: *The critic said that the actress's performance in the play was mediocre.*

me·nag·er·ie (mə năj′ə rē *or* mə năzh′ə rē) *n.* A collection of animals kept in cages or pens, usually for exhibition: *Because of the unusual animals, many people came to see the menagerie.*

me·te·or·o·log·i·cal (mē′tē ər ə lŏg′ĭ kəl) *adj.* Of or relating to the science that deals with the study of the atmosphere, weather, and climate: *The weather forecaster gave an hourly update of the meteorological conditions at the airport.* — **me′te·or·o·log′i·cal·ly** *adv.*

mon·ar·chy (mŏn′ər kē *or* mŏn′är kē) *n., pl.* **mon·ar·chies.** A government by a ruler who inherits the position, such as a king or queen: *France was a monarchy until 1789.*

mo·not·o·nous (mə nŏt′n əs) *adj.* **1.** Dull or tiresome because of a lack of variety: *Following the same schedule every day became monotonous.* **2.** Sounded or uttered in the same tone: *Several people fell asleep during the monotonous lecture.* **—mo·not′o·nous·ly** *adv.*

mo·rose (mə rōs′ *or* mô rōs′) *adj.* Bad-tempered, sullen, or gloomy: *After losing to their rivals, the whole tennis team was morose.* **—mo·rose′ly** *adv.* **—mo·rose′ness** *n.*

mull (mŭl) *v.* To think about carefully; ponder: *I mulled over what to pack for the weekend trip.*

mu·ti·late (myōō′l āt′) **mu·ti·lat·ed, mu·ti·lat·ing, mu·ti·lates. 1.** To injure or disfigure seriously, as by cutting off a limb: *The hungry lion mutilated the antelope.* **2.** To damage badly: *The huge truck mutilated the bicycle that was parked in the driveway.* **—mu′ti·la′tion** *n.*

N

nav·i·ga·tion (năv′ĭ gā′shən) *n.* The art or science of directing the course or locating the position of a ship: *Sailors used the position of the stars in the navigation of their ships.* **—nav′i·ga′tion·al** *adj.*

nour·ish·ment (nûr′ĭsh mənt *or* nŭr′ĭsh mənt) *n.* Something that provides substances necessary for life and growth; food: *During the winter it is important to provide nourishment for the birds.*

no·ve·na (nō vē′ nə) *n., pl.* **no·ve·nas** or **no·ve·nae** (nō vē′ nē). In the Roman Catholic Church an observance that consists of nine days of prayers and devotions.

O

o·cean·og·ra·phy (ō′ shə nŏg′ rə fē) *n.* The scientific study and exploration of the environment of the ocean and its plants and animals: *I want to study oceanography because I love the ocean and its animals.*

oc·tag·o·nal (ŏk tăg′ ə nəl) *adj.* Having eight sides and eight angles: *A stop sign has an octagonal shape.*

o·mit (ō mĭt′) *v.* **o·mit·ted, o·mit·ting, o·mits.** To leave out; fail to include: *Unfortunately, I omitted my friend's name from the guest list.* — **o·mis′ sion** *n.*

op·tion (ŏp′ shən) *n.* **1.** A choice: *My only option is to cut the grass.* **2.** The right to choose: *We had the option of walking or taking the bus.*

or·nate (ôr nāt′) *adj.* Highly decorated, often with much ornamentation: *The ornate bowl was so valuable that it was for display only.* —**or·nate′ ly** *adv.* —**or·nate′ ness** *n.*

o·ver·head (ō′ vər hĕd′) *n.* The general expenses of running a business, such as rent, taxes, electricity, and heating: *The business had so much overhead that it was not profitable.*

P

pa·le·on·tol·o·gist (pā′ lē ŏn tŏl′ ə jĭst) *n.* A scientist who specializes in the study of fossils and ancient forms of life: *The paleontologist spent months looking for a fossil of a baby dinosaur.*

par·a·ble (păr ə bəl) *n.* A short, simple story that teaches a truth or moral lesson: *The parable in the book taught that lying is harmful.*

par·a·graph (păr′ ə grăf′) *n.* A distinct part of a piece of writing that begins on a new, usually indented line and consists of one or more sentences on one particular subject or idea: *The teacher said to write a paragraph about a favorite sport.*

par·a·le·gal (păr′ ə lē′ gəl) *adj.* Of, relating to, or being a person who is trained to assist a lawyer and perform certain legal tasks but is not licensed to practice law: *The lawyer asked the paralegal to research cases in the law library.*

pa·ral·y·sis (pə răl′ ĭ sĭs) *n., pl.* **pa·ral·y·ses** (pə ral′ĭ sēz′). **1.** The loss of movement or sensations in a part of the body: *The stroke caused paralysis in Grandma's right arm.* **2.** A state of inactivity or inability to act, move, or function normally: *The sight of the huge animal caused paralysis in the young child.*

par·a·med·ic (păr′ ə mĕd′ ĭk) *n.* A person who is trained to assist a doctor or give emergency medical treatment: *The paramedics gave emergency treatment to the accident victims.* — **par′ a·med′ i·cal** *adj.*

par·a·pher·na·lia (păr′ ə fər nāl′ yə) *pl. n. (used with a singular or plural verb).* **1.** Personal belongings: *We packed all our paraphernalia in two suitcases.* **2.** Equipment used in a particular activity: *The carpenter carried a lot of paraphernalia in his toolbox.*

par·a·pro·fes·sion·al (păr′ ə prə fĕsh′ ə nəl) *n.* A person who is trained to assist a professional but is not licensed in that profession: *Schools often have paraprofessionals who assist teachers.*

par·a·site (păr′ ə sīt′) *n.* **1.** An animal or plant that lives on a different kind of animal or plant from which it gets its food. **2.** A person who gets support from or lives off another but gives nothing in return: *Because the boy was a parasite, he had few friends.*

par·tic·i·pate (pär tĭs′ ə pāt′) *v.* **par·tic·i·pat·ed, par·tic·i·pat·ing, par·tic·i·pates.** To take part in or have a share with others: *Our class will participate in the charity drive.* —**par·tic′ i·pa tion** *n.*

pen·e·trate (pĕn′ ĭ trāt′) *v.* **pen·e·trat·ed, pen·e·trat·ing, pen·e·trates. 1.** To pass into or through, especially by force; pierce: *The light from the flashlight penetrated the darkness.* **2.** To enter into and spread throughout: *The damp cold penetrated my light jacket.*

pe·rim·e·ter (pə rĭm′ ĭ tər) *n.* **1.** The outer boundary of a figure or area: *There was a stone fence on the perimeter of the field.* **2.** The length of such a boundary: *The perimeter of the room is 34 feet.*

pe·ri·od·ic (pĭr′ ē ŏd′ ĭk) *adj.* **1.** Occurring or happening at regular intervals: *The periodic chiming of the clock was hourly.* **2.** Happening from time to time or irregularly: *We looked forward to the periodic appearance of the hummingbird.* — **pe′ ri·od′ i·cal·ly** *adv.*

per·mis·si·ble (pər mĭs′ ə bəl) *adj.* Permitted; allowable: *The teacher said it was permissable to look at our notes during the test.*

per·sist·ent (pər sĭs′ tənt) *adj.* **1.** Refusing to give up in spite of difficulty: *The persistent scientist finally discovered a cure for the rare disease.* **2.** Continuing; lasting: *The persistent dripping of the faucet was annoying.* —**per·sis′ ent·ly** *adv.*

per·son·i·fy (pər sŏn′ ə fī′) *v.* **per·son·fied, per·son·fy·ing, per·son·i·fies. 1.** To be the perfect example of something; typify: *Sam's attention to every detail personifies a perfectionist.* **2.** To represent a thing as having human qualities.

pet·ty (pĕt′ē) *adj.* **pet·ti·er, pet·ti·est. 1.** Of little importance: *Although the complaints were petty, the supervisor promised to take care of the problems.* **2.** Mean, spiteful, or narrow-minded: *The petty girl made a point of telling me about every mistake I made.* —**pet′ti·ly** *adv.* —**pet′ti·ness** *n.*

phar·aoh (fâr′ō *or* fā′rō) *n.* A king of ancient Egypt: *The pharaohs inherited their positions.*

pin·na·cle (pĭn′ə kəl) *n.* **1.** The highest point: *Winning the award was the pinnacle of the author's career.* **2.** A high, pointed formation, as a mountain peak.

pique (pēk) *v.* **piqued, piqu·ing, piques. 1.** To excite; arouse: *The article about animal emotions piqued my curiosity.* **2.** To arouse anger or resentment: *My lack of friendliness piqued my friend.* —*n.* Resentment or irritation caused by having one's feelings hurt.

plat·i·tude (plăt′ĭ tōōd′ *or* plăt′ĭ tyōōd′) *n.* A dull, commonplace, or overused remark or expression: *The editorial cartoon made fun of the candidate's use of platitudes.*

po·tent (pōt′nt) *adj.* Having strength; powerful; effective: *The potent medicine cured the disease.*

pre·cise (prĭ sīs′) *adj.* **1.** Exact in measurement or amount: *The cake will not taste good unless it is baked at the precise temperature stated in the recipe.* **2.** Exact; very accurate. *The witness gave a precise statement about what had happened.* —**pre·cise ly** *adv.* —**pre·cise ness** *n.*

pred·e·ces·sor (prĕd′ĭ sĕs′ər *or* prē′dĭ sĕs′ər) *n.* A person who comes before another as in an office or position: *The secretary's predecessor left detailed notes about the job.*

prej·u·dice (prĕj′ə dĭs) *n.* **1.** An unfavorable opinion or judgment formed beforehand without facts or knowledge: *The judge asked the jurors if they had any prejudice about the case.* **2.** Hatred of a particular group based on race, religion, etc.; bigotry: *Prejudice is unacceptable in the United States.*

pre·scribe (prĭ skrīb′) *v.* **pre·scribed, pre·scrib·ing, pre·scribes. 1.** To give or set down as a rule or course of action to be followed: *The school district prescribed the mathematics curriculum.* **2.** To order the use of a medicine or cure: *The doctor prescribed an antibiotic to stop the infection.*

prey (prā) *n.* **1.** An animal hunted or killed for food: *The hawk's prey was a mouse.* **2.** A victim. —*v.* To hunt or kill other animals for food: *The fox preyed on smaller animals for food.*

priv·y (prĭv′ē) *adj.* Having secret or private knowledge of something: *Only Fred's closest friends were privy to the details of the surprise party.*

pro·fi·cien·cy (prə fĭsh′ən sē) *n., pl.* **pro·fi·cien·cies.** The quality or state of being highly skilled; skill; competence: *The gymnast's proficiency earned her a medal.*

prom·e·nade (prŏm′ə nād′ *or* prŏm′ə näd′) *v.* **prom·e·nad·ed, prom·e·nad·ing, prom·e·nades.** To go on a leisurely walk; stroll: *Our whole family promenades through the neighborhood on summer evenings.* —*n.* A leisurely walk, especially in a public place.

pro·pose (prə pōz′) *v.* **pro·posed, pro·pos·ing, pro·pos·es.** To offer for consideration, discussion, or acceptance; suggest: *The children proposed that the family go camping.*

pros·per·ous (prŏs′pər əs) *adj.* Successful; wealthy; thriving: *The prosperous farmer donated food to the poor.* —**pros′per·ous·ly** *adv.*

pun (pŭn) *n.* A humorous play on words using the similarity of the sounds: *Shakespeare often used puns in his plays.*

pun·gent (pŭn′jənt) *adj.* Sharp, strong, stinging, or biting to the taste or smell: *The pungent odor of the burning tires made people sick.* —**pun′gen·cy** *n.* —**pun′gent·ly** *adv.*

pur·sue (pər sōō′) *v.* **pur·sued, pur·su·ing, pur·sues. 1.** To chase in order to overcome or capture: *The police pursued the robber.* **2.** To strive to accomplish: *I plan to pursue a career.*

Q

quad·ru·ple (kwŏ drōō′pəl *or* kwŏ drŭp′əl) *v.* **quad·ru·pled, quad·ru·pling, quad·ru·ples.** To make or become four times as great: *The company's profits quadrupled in two years.* —*adj.* **1.** Consisting of four parts. **2.** Four times as great.

R

reap (rēp) *v.* **1.** To receive as a reward or result of effort: *People reap many benefits from an education.* **2.** To cut (grain) for harvest.

re·cant (rĭ kănt′) *v.* To take back a statement, belief, or opinion, especially formally or publicly: *The talk-show host recanted his statement about the football player.*

reek (rēk) *v.* To give off a strong, bad odor: *After swimming in the muddy pond, the dog reeked.* —*n.* A strong, bad odor.

re·gal (rē′gəl) *adj.* Of or related to royalty: *a regal crown.*

re·main (rĭ mān′) *v.* **1.** To stay behind or in the same place: *We remained at the stadium for an hour after the game.* **2.** To be left over: *The chimney is all that remains of the house after the fire.*

3. To continue unchanged: *The men remained friends for sixty years.*

re·mit·tance (rĭ **mĭt′** ns) *n.* **1.** Money sent to someone as a payment: *I included a check as my remittance for the tickets.* **2.** The act of sending money.

rem·nant (rĕm′ nənt) *n.* **1.** What is left over: *The survivors of the tornado found few remnants of their possessions.* **2.** The cloth or carpet that is left over from the cutting of a bigger piece.

ren·e·gade (rĕn′ ĭ gād′) *n.* **1.** An outlaw: *The renegade was convicted of his crimes.* **2.** A person who abandons or turns against a cause, party, or group in favor of another: *The politician was a renegade who started his own party.*

re·pen·tance (rĭ **pĕn′** təns) *n.* **1.** Sorrow or regret for what one has done, especially for a sin or wrongdoing: *I felt repentance for hurting my friend's feelings.* **2.** The act or process of feeling sorrow or regret for what one has done.

rep·u·ta·tion (rĕp′ yə **tā′** shən) *n.* The judgment or estimation others make of something or someone: *She had a reputation as a fine speaker.*

re·quire (rĭ **kwīr′**) *v.* **re·quired, re·quir·ing, re·quires. 1.** To demand or insist upon: *The teacher requires a note explaining any absence.* **2.** To need: *The sick kitten requires medical assistance.*

req·ui·site (rĕk′ wĭ zĭt) *adj.* Essential; necessary: *The requisite practice for the concert improved everyone's playing.* —*n.* Something that is essential: *A good conductor is a requisite for a successful band.*

re·scind (rĭ **sĭnd′**) *v.* To revoke, cancel, or repeal: *Congress rescinded the law that required a 55-mile-per-hour speed limit on interstate highways.* —**re·scind′ er** *n.*

res·er·voir (rĕz′ ər vwär′ *or* rĕz′ ər vwôr′) *n.* A place where water is stored: *The city reservoir needed repairs because it was leaking.*

re·sis·tance (rĭ **zĭs′** təns) *n.* **1.** The act of withstanding, opposing, or not yielding to: *The army's resistance to the attackers saved the city.* **2.** The ability or power to keep from getting a disease.

re·tal·i·ate (rĭ **tăl′** ē āt′) *v.* **re·tal·i·at·ed, re·tal·i·at·ing, re·tal·i·ates.** To return or repay like for like, especially evil for evil or injury for injury: *When Cindy told on her brother, he retaliated by telling on her.* —**re·tal′ i·a′ tion** *n.* —**re·tal′ i·a·to′ ry** *adj.*

re·tract (rĭ **trăkt′**) *v.* **1.** To take back; withdraw (a statement, promise, etc.): *The senator had to retract his accusation against his opponent.* **2.** To pull or draw back in: *My cat retracts her claws when she purrs.* —**re·tract′ a·ble** *adj.*

re·vers·i·ble (rĭ **vûr′** sə bəl) *adj.* **1.** Capable of being turned around, upside down, inside out, or changed to the opposite: *The jury's decision may be reversible if it is appealed.* **2.** Wearable or usable on either side: *Because the jacket is reversible, I can wear it with twice as many clothes.*

re·vert (rĭ **vûrt′**) *v.* To go back to a former condition, practice, belief, or subject: *When her brother was born, the toddler reverted to acting like a baby.*

rile (rīl) *v.* **riled, ril·ing, riles.** To annoy, irritate, or anger: *Joe riled his sister by pulling her hair.*

S

sage (sāj) *adj.* **sag·er, sag·est.** Wise or showing sound judgment: *The young athletes listened to the sage advice of the professional player.* —*n.* A person who is very wise.

saun·ter (sôn′ tər) *v.* To walk at a slow, leisurely pace: *Since we had all day, we sauntered from one shop to the next.*

sa·vor (sā′ vər) *v.* To enjoy the taste or smell of: *I savored the birthday cake.* —*n.* A particular taste or smell of something.

schol·ar·ship (skŏl′ ər shĭp′) *n.* **1.** Knowledge gained by study; learning: *The teachers were impressed by the scholarship of the new student.* **2.** A gift of money given to a student to help pay for the cost of studies.

scho·las·tic (skə **lăs′** tĭk) *adj.* Of or relating to schools, scholars, or education: *The university is known for its high scholastic standards.*

scorch (skôrch) *v.* **scorched, scorch·ing, scorch·es. 1.** To burn slightly so as to affect the appearance or taste of: *The hot temperature of the burner scorched the gravy.* **2.** To dry up or wither with high heat: *The hot sun scorched the tender vegetables.*

scrawl (skrôl) *v.* To write or draw carelessly or hastily: *The young child scrawled all over the wall.*

scru·ti·ny (skrōōt′ n ē) *n., pl.* **scru·ti·nies.** A close, careful, or critical examination or study: *The accountant conducted a scrutiny of the financial books after the robbery.*

scur·ry (skûr′ ē *or* skŭr′ ē) *v.* **scur·ried, scur·ry·ing, scur·ries.** To move hurriedly; dash; scamper: *The kittens scurried around the yard.*

seis·mo·graph (sīz′ mə grăf′) *n.* An instrument that detects and records the location, direction, duration, and intensity of earthquakes: *The seismograph registered an earthquake even though most people could not feel it.*

sem·i·nar (sĕm′ ə när′) *n.* A small group of students studying and doing research under the supervision of a professor: *The students taking the seminar were all interested in learning about Mars.*

sem·i·nar·y (**sĕm′**ə nĕr ē) *n., pl.* **sem·i·nar·ies.**
1. A school that trains students to be ministers, priests, or rabbis: *The students at the seminary study religious subjects.* **2.** A school of higher learning, especially a private or boarding school for girls.

ser·rat·ed (**sĕr′**ā tĭd) *adj.* Having jagged or rough, sharp edges as a saw or leaf: *The knife had a serrated blade.*

sex·tet (sĕk **stĕt′**) *n.* **1.** A group of six persons or things: *The sextet of friends went everywhere together.* **2.** A musical group consisting of six performers. **3.** A musical composition for six performers.

shod·dy (**shŏd′**ē) *adj.* **shod·di·er, shod·di·est.** Of poor quality; inferior: *The shoddy shirt fell apart after only one washing.*

shriv·el (**shrĭv′**əl) *v.* To shrink and wrinkle: *The rose petals shriveled and fell off the plant.*

si·es·ta (sē **ĕs′**tə) *n.* A midday or afternoon rest or nap: *After my siesta I was fully rested.*

sight (sīt) *n.* The ability or act of seeing: *They hoped the surgery would restore the woman's sight.*

site (sīt) *n.* The place where something was, is, or will be located: *The site of the new hotel is next to the convention center.*

skir·mish (**skûr′**mĭsh) *n.* **1.** A brief or minor battle between small bodies of troops: *The skirmish was a preview of a larger battle to come.* **2.** An unimportant conflict. —*v.* **skir·mished, skir·mish·ing, skir·mish·es.** To take part in a brief or minor conflict.

slea·zy (**slē′**zē) *adj.* **slea·zi·er, slea·zi·est.**
1. Corrupt; disreputable: *The sleazy salesperson promised anything just to make a sale.* **2.** Shabby; cheap: *The sleazy restaurant didn't have many customers.* —**slea′zi·ly** *adv.* —**slea′zi·ness** *n.*

slip·shod (**slĭp′**shŏd′) *adj.* **1.** Carelessly done or made: *The teacher gave a low grade to the slipshod project.* **2.** Untidy: *Our appearance was slipshod after we camped in the woods for a week.*

smor·gas·bord (**smôr′**gəs bôrd′) *n.* A large variety of food arranged on a table so people serve themselves: *The smorgasbord included many different appetizers, meat dishes, vegetables, and desserts.*

so·journ (**sō′**jûrn′ *or* sō **jûrn′**) *v.* To stay in a place for a short time: *Lewis and Clark sojourned with various Indian tribes during their journey west.* —*n.* A short stay. —**so′journ′er** *n.*

son·net (**sŏn′**ĭt) *n.* A poem that has fourteen lines and one of several rhyme schemes: *Although sonnets are short, they can be very meaningful.*

squal·id (**skwŏl′**ĭd) *adj.* Miserable; wretched; disgusting: *Squalid living conditions often cause sickness and disease.* —**squal′id·ly** *adv.* —**squal′id·ness** *n.*

stan·za (**stăn′**zə) *n.* A group of lines in a poem usually arranged with a common pattern of meter and rhyme: *I memorized the first stanza of the poem.*

stench (stĕnch) *n.* A strong, bad smell: *The stench of the rotten eggs was unbearable.*

strive (strīv) *v.* **strove, striv·en** *or* **strived, striv·ing, strives.** To try hard; make a great effort: *The orchestra strove to play the Mozart concerto perfectly.*

sub·mit (səb **mĭt′**) *v.* **sub·mit·ted, sub·mit·ting, sub·mits. 1.** To present something for consideration: *More than 50 people submitted applications for the job.* **2.** To give up; surrender: *The losers submitted themselves to their conquerors.* —**sub·mit′tal** *n.*

sub·scribe (səb **scrīb′**) *v.* **sub·scribed, sub·scrib·ing, sub·scribes. 1.** To agree to receive and pay for a certain number of things, such as a magazine: *I decided to subscribe to the news magazine for two years.* **2.** To promise to contribute a certain amount of money: *The zoo asked for people to subscribe to its conservation fund.* —**sub·scrib′er** *n.*

sub·si·dize (**sŭb′**sĭ dīz′) *v.* **sub·si·dized, sub·si·diz·ing, sub·si·diz·es.** To aid, assist, or support with a grant of money: *A tax increase was necessary in order to subsidize the cost of the new domed stadium.* —**sub′si·diz′er** *n.*

su·perb (soo **pûrb′**) *adj.* Excellent: *The superb television show won nine awards.* —**su·perb′ly** *adv.*

sym·bol·ism (**sĭm′**bə lĭz′ əm) *n.* The use of something to represent something else, such as an idea, in religion, art, or literature: *I understood the symbolism in the poem after the teacher explained it.*

syn·thet·ic (sĭn **thĕt′**ĭk) *adj.* Not natural; artificial: *Polyester is a synthetic fabric.* —**syn·thet′i·cal·ly** *adv.*

T

ta·boo (tə **boo′** *or* tă **boo′**) *n., pl.* **ta·boos.** A prohibition against certain things based on social, cultural, or conventional reasons: *There is a taboo against wearing hats in the building.* —*adj.* Prohibited or forbidden from use or mention: *That topic is taboo in class.*

tan·trum (**tăn′**trəm) *n.* A sudden outburst of bad temper, anger, or rage: *Emily threw a tantrum when Alice took her toy.*

tar·ry (tăr′ē) *v.* **tar·ried, tar·ry·ing, tar·ries.** To delay in starting, acting, or doing something: *Even though we had work to do, we tarried at the bookstore.*

tart (tärt) *adj.* **1.** Sharp in taste; sour: *The recipe said to use tart apples.* **2.** Sharp or biting in tone or meaning: *The senator gave a tart reply to the reporter's question.* —**tart′ ly** *adv.* —**tart′ ness** *n.*

taunt (tônt) *v.* **1.** To sarcastically mock or criticize with insults: *It is poor sportsmanship to taunt the opposing team.* **2.** To irritate by teasing: *The mean children taunted the dog.* —*n.* An insulting remark.

tem·per·ate (tĕm′pər ĭt *or* tĕm′prĭt) *adj.* Having mild or moderate temperatures that are neither too hot nor too cold: *Animals are abundant in a temperate climate.*

thaw (thô) *v.* To melt: *When the temperature rises above 32° F., ice will thaw.*

the·o·rize (thē′ə rīz′ *or* thîr′īz) *v.* **the·o·rized, the·o·riz·ing, the·o·riz·es.** To form an explanation based on an assumption or guess: *Because there were no survivors, the investigators could only theorize about what caused the plane crash.*

thrive (thrīv) *v.* **thrived** or **throve, thrived** or **thriv·en, thriv·ing, thrives. 1.** To grow vigorously or very well: *Roses will thrive in fertile soil.* **2.** To be successful; prosper: *When gold was discovered, the town thrived.*

to·pog·ra·phy (tə pŏg′rə fē) *n., pl.* **to·pog·ra·phies.** The detailed description or drawing of the physical features of a place or area, such as hills, valleys, rivers, and lakes: *It is a good idea to know the topography of a region before beginning a long camping trip.*

trag·e·dy (trăj′ĭ dē) *n., pl.* **trag·e·dies.** A serious play with a sad ending in which the main character meets with great misfortune, especially as a result of a personal flaw or weakness: *Shakespeare wrote the tragedy* Julius Caesar.

trait (trāt) *n.* A distinguishing feature, quality, or characteristic, as of a person's character: *Honesty was one of George Washington's traits.*

tran·script (trăn′skrĭpt′) *n.* A written or typewritten copy: *The jurors read the transcript of the trial.*

trans·form (trăns fôrm′) *v.* **1.** To change in form, shape, or appearance: *The ugly duckling was transformed into a beautiful swan.* **2.** To change the condition, character, nature, or function of: *The warm sun transformed the ice into water.*

treach·er·ous (trĕch′ər əs) *adj.* **1.** Dangerous: *The roads were treacherous after the ice storm.* **2.** Likely to betray a trust; disloyal: *The treacherous girl told secrets that she had promised to keep.*

triv·i·al (trĭv′ē əl) *adj.* Of little importance; insignificant: *Even though my part in the play was trivial, I rehearsed for hours.* —**triv′ i·al′ i·ty,** *n.* —**triv′ i·al·ly** *adv.*

tru·an·cy (trōō′ən sē) *n., pl.* **tru·an·cies.** The act or practice of being absent without permission: *The student missed a test because of truancy.*

tur·bu·lent (tûr′byə lənt) *adj.* Causing or marked by violence, great disturbance, or disorder; not calm or smooth: *The hurricane caused the ocean to be turbulent.*

ty·pog·ra·phy (tī pŏg′rə fē) *n., pl.* **ty·pog·ra·phies. 1.** The art, act, or process of setting and printing with type or a movable press: *The man had to learn typography to work in the print shop.* **2.** The appearance of printed matter.

U

un·e·quiv·o·cal (ŭn′ĭ kwĭv′ə kəl) *adj.* Having no doubt; clear and easily understood: *The unequivocal answer required no more explanation.* —**un′ e·quiv′ o·cal·ly** *adv.*

u·ni·for·mi·ty (yōō′nə fôr′mĭ tē) *n., pl.* **u·ni·form·i·ties.** The state, quality, or instance of always being the same; sameness: *Marching bands strive for uniformity in their steps.*

un·in·hab·it·a·ble (ŭn′ĭn hăb′ĭ tə bəl) *adj.* Unfit to be lived in: *The house was in such poor condition that it was uninhabitable.* —**un·in·hab′ it·a·bil′ i·ty** *n.*

un·re·mark·a·ble (ŭn′rĭ mär′kə bəl) *adj.* Ordinary; common: *The unremarkable day was just like any other day.* —**un′ re·mark′ a·bly** *adv.*

un·seat (ŭn sēt′) *v.* To remove from an office or position: *The majority of voters want to unseat the senator.*

ur·gen·cy (ûr′jən sē) *n., pl.* **ur·gen·cies.** The quality or condition of calling for immediate action or attention: *The flu epidemic caused doctors to stress the urgency for people to be vaccinated.*

u·til·ize (yōōt′l īz′) *v.* **u·til·ized, u·til·iz·ing, u·til·iz·es.** Make use of, especially for practical or profitable purposes: *We learned to utilize the microscope in science.* —**u′ ti·li·za′ tion** *n.*

V

va·gran·cy (vā′grən sē) *n., pl.* **va·gran·cies.** The condition of being a person without a regular home or employment who wanders from place to place and may be a public nuisance: *The man was arrested for vagrancy because he was bothering people in the city park.*

veg·e·ta·tion (vĕj′ĭ **tā**′shən) *n*. Plant life: *The vegetation in the jungle is different from plant life in the desert.*

ven·ture (**vĕn**′chər) *n*. **1.** To make a daring journey: *On our vacation we ventured into the mountains.* **2.** To expose to risk or danger of loss: *The investor ventured all his money in one company's stock.* —*n*. A risky or dangerous undertaking.

ver·bose (vər **bōs**′) *adj*. Using too many words; wordy: *The verbose paragraph was very repetitive.* —**ver·bose**′**ly** *adv*. —**ver·bos**′**i·ty** *n*.

ver·sion (**vûr**′zhən) *n*. **1.** An account or description from a particular point of view: *The two witnesses' versions of the accident were quite different.* **2.** A different or changed form of something: *The second version of the movie is better than the first version.*

ver·sus (**vûr**′səs or **vûr**′sĕz) *prep*. **1.** Against: *When it is our team versus our rival school's team, nobody is sure who will win.* **2.** In contrast to or as a different choice: *I like the hot weather of summer versus the cold weather of winter.*

vig·or (**vĭg**′ər) *n*. Energy, strength, vitality: *The basketball player's vigor is due to proper diet and exercise.*

vi·tal (**vīt**′l) *adj*. **1.** Essential; very important: *The store provided vital information about getting on the internet.* **2.** Necessary for life: *Breathing is vital to a mammal's life.* —**vi**′**tal·ly** *adv*.

vul·ner·a·ble (**vŭl**′nər ə bəl) *adj*. **1.** Easily harmed or injured: *Because the rabbit's nest was destroyed, its babies were vulnerable.* **2.** Able to be hurt emotionally: *The girl was vulnerable because she was new to the school.* —**vul**′**ner·a·bil**′**i·ty** *n*. —**vul**′**ner·a·bly** *adv*.

W

wa·ver (**wā**′vər) *v*. **1.** To show doubt or uncertainty: *From the time Chung was a little boy, he never wavered from his goal to be a doctor.* **2.** To sway back and forth: *The tall grass wavered in the wind.* —**wa**′**ver·er** *n*.

whiff (wĭf) *n*. **1.** A slight, passing odor or smell: *I got a whiff of baking bread as I passed the bakery.* **2.** A sudden slight puff or gust of wind: *The whiff of air gently blew the leaves.* —*v*. **1.** To blow gently. **2.** To breathe.

won·drous (**wŭn**′drəs) *adj*. Wonderful: *The sun setting in the west and the full moon coming up in the east were wondrous sights.* —**won**′**drous·ly** *adv*.

Standardized Test Practice

In lessons 1 to 36, you have concentrated on building vocabulary, a skill that is an important aid in reading comprehension. However, the competent reader must master a variety of other skills. These include the following:

- **Identifying main and subordinate ideas**—deciding what the most important idea in the selection is and what items support that idea

  Examples:
  Main idea   The ancient Maya had a fascinating culture.
  Subordinate   The ancient Maya developed irrigation.
                     They created an accurate calendar.
                     Mayan artists produced sculptures, painting, and jewelry.

- **Deciding on an appropriate title**—choosing a title that is closely related to the main idea of a selection

- **Drawing inferences**—coming to a conclusion that is not directly stated but is based on information given

  Example:
  If someone is breathing hard, you can infer that the person has been running.

- **Locating details**—scanning a selection to find the answer to a specific question

The following pages will give you a chance to practice the skills you use when you read. The questions they contain are the kinds of questions you will be asked to answer on a standardized test.

The reading selections include passages from science and social studies texts as well as informative essays and short narratives.

Reread the selection "The Teapot Dome Affair" on page 15. Then circle the letter of the answer that BEST completes each of the following sentences.

1. The subject of "The Teapot Dome Affair" is

   A. a problem with imports of tea from Asia.

   B. political corruption involving oil resources.

   C. the misuse of heirloom china in the White House.

   D. a family scandal involving a member of the Cabinet.

2. Politicians who took part in *extortion* activities were involved in

   A. forgery.

   B. burglary.

   C. blackmail.

   D. counterfeiting.

3. Private oil interests were opposed to the petroleum reserve policy because

   A. they were eager to profit from the control of oil resources.

   B. they planned to use the resources for the good of the general public.

   C. they wanted to relieve government agencies of unnecessary pressure.

   D. they thought that the government lacked the expertise to manage the resources.

4. From this selection, you can infer that

   A. oil is a very valuable commodity.

   B. Albert B. Fall was an honest official.

   C. scandals and corruption are rare in governments.

   D. Warren G. Harding would not tolerate illegal activities by his cabinet members.

5. One who takes part in a disagreement may be referred to as a(n)

   A. associate.

   B. disputant.

   C. conspirator.

   D. investigator.

Reread the selection "The Tale of Osebo's Drum" on page 43. Then circle the letter of the correct answer to each of the following questions.

1. Which statement describes the way this selection is narrated?

   A. It is told by a main character in the story.

   B. It is told by a minor character in the story.

   C. It is told by someone outside the story who simply presents the events.

   D. It is told by someone outside the story who presents the events and reacts to them.

2. How did the other animals react to Turtle's success?

   A. They were very surprised.

   B. They accused him of cheating.

   C. They were jealous of his success.

   D. They showed their pleasure by congratulating him.

3. How did Turtle trick Osebo the Leopard?

   A. Turtle persuaded Osebo to bring the drum to the Sky God.

   B. Turtle pretended to be dying so that Osebo would bring him back to his home.

   C. Turtle told Osebo that Nyame's drum was so large that Nyame could crawl inside it.

   D. Turtle flattered Osebo by telling him that no one had a drum greater than Leopard's.

4. How did Osebo the Leopard get his spots?

   A. Turtle painted the spots on Osebo.

   B. The Sky God sprinkled Osebo with ashes.

   C. Osebo rolled in blackberries, staining his hide.

   D. Osebo stumbled into Sky God's fire and scorched himself.

5. What does the word *apprehensive*, in the second paragraph, mean?

   A. aware

   B. fearful

   C. delighted

   D. nonchalant

Reread the selection "Giganotosaurus" on page 71. Then circle the letter of the BEST choice to complete each statement.

1. Scientists have concluded that *Giganotosaurus Carolini* was a meat eater because

    A. there was no other food in the area.

    B. it would have to eat meat to sustain its large size.

    C. its teeth were like those of other meat-eating animals.

    D. skeletons of smaller animals were found near its bones.

2. The most surprising fact about *Giganotosaurus* was that

    A. its bones were discovered by an auto mechanic, not a professional paleontologist.

    B. it was as large as *Tyrannosaurus rex.*

    C. it was found in South America.

    D. its skin was green and pink.

3. *Giganotosaurus Carolini* was discovered

    A. last year.

    B. over 50 years ago.

    C. within the last 25 years.

    D. before *Tyrannosaurus rex* was discovered.

4. The most accurate comparison between *Giganotosaurus* and *T-rex* is that

    A. *T-rex* is larger than *Giganotosaurus.*

    B. *Giganotosaurus* is older and heavier than *T-rex.*

    C. *Giganotosaurus* and *T-rex* roamed the earth at the same time.

    D. *Giganotosaurus* and *T-rex* ate entirely different types of food.

5. The word *attributes,* on line 20, refers to

    A. praises.

    B. qualities.

    C. additions.

    D. expenses.

Reread the selection "World Habitats" on page 113. Then circle the letter of the correct answer to each of the following questions.

1. Which of the earth's biomes is most uninhabitable?

   A. the desert

   B. the African savanna

   C. the continent of Antarctica

   D. the region around the North Pole

2. Why can mountains contain more than one ecological system?

   A. Ecological systems are based on climate, which changes with altitude.

   B. They provide an abundance of food for various types of animals.

   C. They cover much of the earth's surface.

   D. They exist on different continents.

3. Which of the following statements is NOT true?

   A. Although golden eagles and snow leopards are predators, they share an ecological system with foraging animals.

   B. Jungles cover only a small part of the earth's land, but they support the most varieties of plant and animal life.

   C. Plant life in the frozen tundra includes mosses and grasses.

   D. No plants or animals can survive in desert areas.

4. What is the main food supply of animals in the Antarctic region?

   A. air-borne seeds

   B. insects and birds

   C. small grasses and berries

   D. microscopic sea life and zooplankton

5. What does the word *thrives*, in paragraph 3, mean?

   A. fades

   B. exists

   C. prospers

   D. scrapes by

Read the selection below and then answer the questions that follow.

Coming to America

The ship was gigantic! Much as he tried, Giorgio still couldn't find his way around without getting lost. "I guess lost is how I'm going to feel for a while," Giorgio said to himself with a frown. "New friends, new country, new language, new everything!" He sighed and walked outside to the upper deck of the ship.

Giorgio spotted his mother and his aunt Louisa lounging in the warm sunshine. The three had been sailing for a whole week already. They were moving to the United States from Fano, Italy. The year was 1949, and Giorgio Emmanuelle had just turned fourteen. "Don't look so worried, my boy," his mother said. She stroked his hair and smiled at him. Her face looked calm and collected, but Giorgio couldn't help feeling anxious. In just a few short weeks he would be starting a new school in America! How would the other kids treat him?

Just after World War II, Giorgio's mother decided to move her family out of Italy. In addition to having many relatives living happily in the United States already, Estella Emmanuelle wanted to make a fresh start. Giorgio's well-being was her main priority. Her young boy would have many new and exciting opportunities in the United States!

Suddenly they heard the thunderous blare of a foghorn. Jumping up, Giorgio, his mother, his aunt Louisa, and many of the other European passengers rushed to the guard rails along the side of the ship to see what the commotion was about. Off in the distance was the skyline of New York City!

"Giorgio!" his mother shouted excitedly. "Look at your new home! It is magnificent!" Giorgio couldn't help agreeing as the city came closer and closer. In Italy the architecture was beautiful and historical, but everything in New York City looked modern and fresh. Towering buildings were being constructed right before their eyes. People on the docks in New York City were waving frantically to the passengers on the ship. The passengers were cheering.

As they approached the dock, Giorgio took a deep breath and exhaled slowly. This country was his new home. "There will be many challenges, Mother," he said quietly, as he observed the people bustling about frantically on the pier. "But I am ready for them all!"

Circle the letter of the BEST choice to complete each statement.

1. This story would most likely be found in a book titled
    A. *Historic Italy.*
    B. *The New Americans.*
    C. *Transatlantic Travel.*
    D. *New York Architecture.*

2. There is enough information in the story to tell us that
    A. Giorgio has no cousins.
    B. Giorgio's father was killed in World War II.
    C. Giorgio's mother is older than his Aunt Louisa.
    D. Giorgio is not making the trip to America alone.

3. In the sixth paragraph, the word *frantically* means
    A. sadly.
    B. happily.
    C. lovingly.
    D. excitedly.

4. Giorgio's mother strokes his hair
    A. to straighten it.
    B. to comfort him.
    C. because she is sad about leaving Italy.
    D. because he is disturbing other passengers.

5. Giorgio's mother moved the family to New York mainly to
    A. start a restaurant.
    B. escape World War II.
    C. give her son a better life.
    D. take care of Giorgio's aunt Louisa.

6. The *main* theme of the story is
    A. a boy's feelings about his new life in the United States.
    B. a description of the voyage to the United States from Italy.
    C. the family life of European immigrants to the United States.
    D. a comparison of the architecture of Fano, Italy, and New York City.

The First Day of Basketball

1   Chris slowly walked out onto the court. He stared at his sneakers, imagining that the other kids wouldn't notice him as long as he pretended not to notice them. Today was the first day of basketball practice in gym class. Chris could picture himself falling flat on his face as he attempted to run and dribble at the same time. Mr. Henson, the gym teacher, divided the last group of boys into two teams and told them to take their positions on the court. There were four other boys on his team, so it was likely that he wouldn't even have to touch the ball.

2   As soon as Mr. Henson blew his whistle, the gymnasium was alive with the sounds of cheering and the squeaking of the hardwood floor. Chris stood stiffly on the court as the other boys dashed around him. Chris watched his teammates nervously, afraid that someone might accidentally pass him the ball.

3   Gary Parker could see that Chris looked anxious, but he decided to pass Chris the ball. Chris caught it with an unconscious reflex.

4   For a moment, Chris just stood in the middle of the court holding the ball. "Run! Run!" his teammates shouted from all sides.

5   Before Chris realized what he was doing, he was racing down the court, effortlessly dribbling the ball at his side. "Shoot! Shoot!" his teammates were now shouting. Chris tossed the ball up into the air. His eyes widened, and his mouth hung open, as the ball swished through the basket.

Circle the letter of the BEST choice to complete each statement.

1. Gary probably decides to pass the ball to Chris because
   A. Chris is a fair basketball player.
   B. Chris told Gary to pass the ball to him.
   C. Chris needs someone to be confident in him.
   D. Chris is standing directly beneath the basket.

2. The passage shows that
   A. Chris is failing gym class.
   B. Chris is on the varsity basketball team.
   C. Chris does not think that he is a very good basketball player.
   D. Chris has been looking forward to playing basketball all year.

3. At the end of the story, Chris's eyes widen and his mouth hangs open because
   A. he is getting sick.
   B. he is amazed that he has made a basket.
   C. he is having some trouble seeing the ball.
   D. he is worried about what his teammates think of him.

4. The hardwood floor is squeaking because
   A. the boys are running across   C. there is a mouse loose
      it in their sneakers.   in the gym.
   B. there is a loose floorboard.   D. Chris ran too slowly.

5. Mr. Henson blows his whistle
   A. because Chris has gotten a basket.   C. to divide the class into teams.
   B. to get the game started.   D. to stop the game.

6. Gary concludes that Chris looks anxious because Chris
   A. stands stiffly on the court as the other boys dash around him.
   B. fell as he attempted to run and dribble at the same time.
   C. is afraid that someone might pass him the ball.
   D. is staring at his sneakers.

7. In paragraph 4, *reflex* means
   A. reflected light.
   B. a mirrored image.
   C. a conscious way of thinking.
   D. an unconscious response to a stimulus.

Read the selection below and then answer the questions that follow.

Jim Thorpe

1   As 1999 drew to a close, well-known sports reporters were asked to vote for the greatest athlete of the twentieth century. At the top of the list of fifty were names everybody knows: Michael Jordan, Babe Ruth, Mohammed Ali. Only a few spots lower on the list, however, was a name many Americans may have forgotten: Jim Thorpe.

2   Who was the sports hero the writers named the seventh-greatest athlete of the twentieth century? Jim Thorpe was a star early in the 1900s, long before television made household names of American sports stars. Most people who saw him perform are no longer alive, so he is remembered today only by serious fans of sports history.

3   Even so, nearly everyone in 1912 knew Jim Thorpe, a Native American. That was the year he dominated the Olympics in Sweden by winning two multievent competitions, the pentathlon and the decathlon. Thorpe won the decathlon by a huge margin. At the end of the competition, the king of Sweden told Jim Thorpe, "Sir, you are the greatest athlete in the world."

4   After excelling in many sports in college, Thorpe played both major-league baseball and professional football. Jim Thorpe's life took a tragic turn, though. In 1913 it was discovered that he had played professional baseball in 1909. Like most poor young athletes, Thorpe had been happy to earn money doing something he loved. Others, however, used false names to protect their amateur status. Because Thorpe had used his own name, his professional career was discovered. At that time, Olympic rules prohibited professional athletes from Olympic competition. Because of this, Thorpe's medals were taken from him, and his records were erased from the record books.

5   Many years later, though, people began to talk again about Jim Thorpe's many achievements. In 1950 sportswriters named him the greatest athlete of the first half of the twentieth century. In 1951 a major motion picture told the story of his life. The greatest recognition, however, came after his death in 1953. In 1963 the Professional Football Hall of Fame opened, and it named Jim Thorpe as one of its first members. Then, in 1982, the Olympic Committee restored Thorpe's medals and records. Seventy years after he had stunned the world with his abilities, Jim Thorpe was once again an Olympic champion.

Circle the letter of the BEST choice to complete each of the following statements.

1. This selection is mostly about
   A. sports heroes.
   B. a great athlete's achievements.
   C. the 1912 Olympics.
   D. the Professional Football Hall of Fame.

2. The author probably wrote this story in order to
   A. argue with sportswriters.
   B. remind readers of a forgotten hero.
   C. compare the abilities of several great athletes.
   D. tell readers how to compete successfully in a decathlon.

3. This selection suggests that Jim Thorpe would be better known today if he had
   A. excelled at basketball.
   B. chosen to concentrate on baseball.
   C. won more medals at the 1912 Olympics.
   D. played at a time when sports were televised.

4. In 1963 Jim Thorpe was inducted into a Hall of Fame for
   A. football.
   B. baseball.
   C. lacrosse.
   D. track and field.

5. In 1913 Thorpe's Olympic medals were taken from him because he
   A. was not an American citizen.
   B. had cheated in several events.
   C. had won prize money for boxing.
   D. had played in professional sports.

6. The following statement is an opinion:
   A. Jim Thorpe played professional baseball in 1909.
   B. Jim Thorpe won the pentathlon and the decathlon in 1912.
   C. It was unfair of the Olympic Committee to take away Jim Thorpe's medals.
   D. In college Jim Thorpe took part in many sports, including swimming and tennis.

7. The word *dominated,* in paragraph 3, means
   A. was superior to all others.
   B. controlled.
   C. withdrew from.
   D. ignored.

Read the selection below and think about how you might apply and interpret the information provided. Then answer the questions that follow.

The Century Ride

A few months ago, I bought a bike. "I will use it to get a little exercise," I thought.

However, when my friend Patrick, a huge bicycling fan, heard that I had bought a bike, he encouraged me to join him for a bike ride. I thought that he meant a leisurely ride around the park. I was wrong. He wanted me to do a "century" ride with him.

A century ride is a bike ride of one hundred miles. Needless to say, I was reluctant to go with Patrick. One hundred miles is a long way for a beginning rider. Patrick, however, promised he would help me train for the ride, so eventually I agreed.

As we trained, Patrick showed me all he knew about biking and preparing for long rides. After several months of training, I felt ready. At least, I hoped I was ready.

When the big day arrived, Patrick explained the route thoroughly and eased my nervousness. Even the other cyclists were helpful, offering encouragement and advice. Everyone told me that I would surprise myself with just how much I could do. I wasn't sure that I believed them, but it turned out that they were correct. I did end up surprising myself, and I finished the century ride.

Patrick had told me everything I needed to know about bicycling, but he had forgotten to tell me one thing—crossing the finish line after riding a bike for one hundred miles is the most rewarding thing in the world. Thanks to Patrick, I now have a memory to last a lifetime.

The questions below ask you to interpret and apply the information from the selection that you just read. Circle the letter before each correct answer.

1. What might people who read this passage learn?

    A. A century ride is a one-hundred-mile bike ride.

    B. Bicyclists ride only one hundred miles at a time.

    C. Bicycling in a century ride is easy and rewarding.

    D. Only professional bicyclists can do a century ride.

2. Look at the chronological list below.

    I. Purchased a bicycle

    II. Agreed to do a century ride with a friend

    III.

    IV. Completed a century ride

    What information about the narrator would BEST fit in number III?

    A. Rode leisurely around the park

    B. Thanked Patrick for his support

    C. Refused to take part in the century ride

    D. Trained for months for the century ride

3. Which of the following provided the MOST help in the narrator's attempt to ride one hundred miles?

    A. Patrick's assistance

    B. a map of the course

    C. a very expensive bike

    D. advice from the other riders

4. What does the narrator mean when he says that he was *reluctant* to agree to the trip?

    A. He looked forward to the challenge.

    B. He didn't want to disappoint Patrick.

    C. He hesitated about attempting such a long trip.

    D. His mother had warned him about getting leg cramps.

Nicaragua

1   Nicaragua lies between the Caribbean Sea and the Pacific Ocean and between Honduras and Costa Rica. At a size of about 50,000 square miles, Nicaragua is the largest country in Central America. It is slightly larger than Louisiana. It contains about 5 million people, most of whom are *mestizos*, people who have both Indian and Spanish ancestors. The population is extremely unevenly distributed. The city of Managua, Nicaragua's capital and largest urban center, is densely populated, as are the country's other cities. In contrast, the coastal region along the Caribbean is sparsely populated because of its hot, wet climate and lack of farmland.

2   Wealth is as unevenly distributed in Nicaragua as the population. A small upper class controls most of the nation's land and its economic power; the rest of the people are very poor. Although free hospital care is offered, there are often no health-care facilities within many miles of farming communities. Education, which is also free, is required for children of elementary school age, but schools in rural areas are few and far apart.

3   The country's economy is based on agriculture, especially on products that are grown for export. Most farming occurs in the western areas of the country, where the climate is good for agriculture and the soil is fertile because of frequent volcanic eruptions. Coffee is the most important export, with cotton, sugar, bananas, and sesame seeds also being of great significance. Corn, some of which is exported, is the most important crop grown for local consumption.

4   Nicaragua has had a tragic history, partly because of frequent earthquakes and volcanoes but also as a result of revolution, war, and corrupt governments. For more than forty years, the country was governed by the Somoza family, which enriched itself at the expense of the citizens. In 1979 this dictatorship was overthrown by a political group known as the Sandinistas. Soon after, a rebel group, the Contras, fought a civil war against the Sandinistas. Today members of various parties are elected democratically to serve in the government.

Circle the letter of the BEST choice to complete each of the following statements.

1. In paragraph 1, the term *mestizo* describes a person's

   A. job.
   B. wealth.
   C. heritage.
   D. political beliefs.

2. In paragraph 1, Nicaragua is compared with Louisiana to describe Nicaragua's

   A. size.
   B. location.
   C. way of life.
   D. population density.

3. The problem that has also provided benefits for Nicaragua is

   A. volcanoes and earthquakes.
   B. political activity and coups.
   C. crowded urban areas.
   D. a hot, wet climate in the east.

4. In paragraph 1, the word *sparsely* shows that the population in the Caribbean coastal region is

   A. fully employed.
   B. the best educated.
   C. the most crowded.
   D. thinly distributed.

5. The sentence in the selection that provides the BEST explanation for the following statement is

   Because prices on the world market for agricultural products are falling, Nicaragua has big economic problems.

   A. "Most farming occurs in the western areas of the country, where the climate for agriculture is good and the soil is fertile because of frequent volcanic eruptions."

   B. "Coffee is the most important export, with cotton, sugar, bananas, and sesame seeds also being of great significance."

   C. "The country's economy is based on agriculture, especially on products that are grown for export."

   D. "Corn, some of which is exported, is the most important crop grown for local consumption."

Read the passages below and answer the questions that follow. Circle the letter of the choice that is the BEST answer to each question.

Soil is a mixture of weathered rock, organic matter, mineral fragments, water, and air. You know that weathering breaks rocks into smaller and smaller particles. Soon plants take root in these small pieces of rock, and worms, insects, and fungi come to live there. These living things add organic matter (such as leaves, twigs, and the remains of dead worms and insects) to the rock fragments. Rock fragments are not soil until plants and animals live in them.

1. What is the main idea of this paragraph?

   A. Fungi live in rocks.

   B. Worms and insects are part of the soil.

   C. Soil needs air and water to produce plants.

   D. Soil is made up of rock, organic materials, water, and air.

2. After the weathering of rock, what happens to help make soil?

   A. Wind blows the soil around.

   B. Large animals dig in the soil.

   C. Plants grow in the rock pieces.

   D. Animals break up small pieces of rock.

[1]Mechanical weathering breaks up rocks but does not change them in other ways. [2]An example of mechanical weathering is the freezing and thawing of water in the cracks of rocks, a process that causes rocks to break apart. [3]Chemical weathering, on the other hand, changes the mineral composition of the rocks and may even dissolve the rocks. [4]An example of chemical weathering is the color change that occurs when certain types of rock come into contact with the oxygen in the air. [5]Both of these weathering processes help create soil.

3. Which sentence states the main idea of this paragraph?

   A. Sentence 1

   B. Sentence 3

   C. Sentence 4

   D. Sentence 5

4. What does the word *particles* mean?

   A. pieces

   B. adverbs

   C. pebbles

   D. the words *a, an,* and *the*

Word List

Word	Lesson	Word	Lesson	Word	Lesson
à la carte	26	confiscate	36	elaborate	5
access	21	conformity	36	embargo	26
acquit	4	consequence	4	embrace	34
adapt	14	conservatory	20	encircle	25
adept	14	consistency	18	endorse	32
administration	4	consolation	1	enterprise	4
adopt	14	conspire	13	entomb	31
adulation	22	consultant	2	epic	17
allocate	4	contemplate	20	epigram	17
allusion	14	convene	10	equator	7
amateur	16	convenience	18	era	7
amble	23	convert	24	estimate	16
ancestor	21	convey	31	exceed	21
anthology	17	corpulent	15	excessive	1
appetizing	35	cower	10	exemplary	11
apprehensive	10	curriculum	20	exhume	16
arduous	22	decathlon	9	expedition	13
aroma	35	deceased	21	expertise	34
array	25	decoy	26	expulsion	1
artisan	28	deface	12	exquisite	11
ascent	19	defect	29	extraordinary	11
associate	4	defective	12	extravagance	18
assume	19	defer	12	extrovert	24
attribute	16	deficient	29	fable	17
banal	32	deformity	12	facade	31
banish	23	degrade	12	fallible	29
barbarous	19	dehydrate	12	fault	29
barren	11	delectable	35	feat	31
barter	2	delegate	1	feeble	29
befall	1	deliberate	10	ferocious	10
bereaved	19	delicate	28	flabbergasted	10
bestir	23	delicatessen	26	foreshadow	17
bestow	1	denounce	12	forethought	1
boisterous	32	dependency	18	forswear	7
bon voyage	26	deplete	12	fragrance	35
breed	34	deprive	12	fraudulent	15
brutish	8	descend	19	frigid	25
capable	29	detain	30	frivolous	11
centenary	9	detention	30	gait	23
cinematographer	6	deteriorate	19	gaudy	5
cite	14	deterrent	12	gilded	31
clamor	32	devoid	25	graphic	6
client	2	dialogue	32	harass	8
coax	32	disarm	33	hexagon	9
coexist	25	disarray	33	hilarious	15
collaborate	36	disavow	33	illumination	31
collate	36	disclaim	33	illusion	14
commemorate	36	disclose	33	immature	27
commerce	2	discredit	33	immoderate	27
commingle	36	disengage	33	impeccable	27
commonplace	5	disheveled	33	impenetrable	27
compensation	2	disillusion	33	impertinence	28
complement	14	disputant	4	improbable	27
compliment	14	distinctive	34	inaccessible	27
compromise	36	distort	33	inaudible	27
concede	10	diversion	24	incoherent	27
conclave	19	diversity	24	incompetent	27
concur	36	doubt	30	indecisive	27
condolence	36	draft	32	indispensable	22
confer	1	dubious	30	inferior	11
confide	36	effectual	29	infiltrate	7

Word List

Word	Lesson	Word	Lesson	Word	Lesson
inflation	2	permissible	21	site	14
infuriated	28	persistent	34	skirmish	8
ingenuity	31	personify	13	sleazy	5
innovative	34	petty	11	slipshod	5
innumerable	25	pharaoh	31	smorgasbord	26
inquisitive	34	pinnacle	31	sojourn	23
inscribe	6	pique	10	sonnet	17
intercede	21	platitude	32	squalid	5
intrigue	22	potent	29	stanza	17
introvert	24	precisely	7	stench	35
intuition	20	predecessor	21	strive	34
inventory	2	prejudice	22	submit	21
invert	24	prescribe	6	subscribe	6
investor	2	prey	16	subsidize	2
invocation	30	privy	13	superb	11
invoke	30	proficiency	18	symbolism	17
irreversible	7	promenade	23	synthetic	7
jaunt	23	propose	19	taboo	26
lacerate	8	prosperous	15	tantrum	8
lambaste	8	pun	17	tarry	23
locale	22	pungent	35	tart	35
lofty	22	pursue	13	taunt	8
loiter	23	quadruple	9	temperate	25
luminous	15	reap	34	thaw	7
lurk	28	recant	32	theorize	16
lustrous	5	reek	35	thrive	25
maim	8	regal	10	topography	6
maneuver	1	remain	30	tragedy	17
marginal	11	remittance	21	trait	34
mausoleum	31	remnant	30	transcript	6
meager	19	renegade	26	transform	28
mediocre	5	repentance	18	treacherous	15
menagerie	26	reputation	28	trivial	11
meteorological	7	require	30	truancy	18
monarchy	9	requisite	30	turbulent	15
monotonous	9	rescind	4	typography	6
morose	15	reservoir	4	unequivocal	13
mull	20	resistance	18	uniformity	9
mutilate	8	retaliate	1	uninhabitable	25
navigation	22	retract	28	unremarkable	13
nourishment	25	reversible	24	unseated	16
novena	9	revert	24	urgency	18
oceanography	6	rile	8	utilize	22
octagonal	9	sage	20	vagrancy	18
omit	21	saunter	23	vegetation	16
option	22	savor	35	venture	13
ornate	5	scholarship	20	verbose	15
overhead	2	scholastic	20	version	24
paleontologist	16	scorch	10	versus	24
parable	3	scrawl	32	vigor	29
paragraph	3	scrutiny	4	vital	13
paralegal	3	scurry	19	vulnerable	29
paralysis	3	seismograph	6	waver	13
paramedic	3	seminar	20	whiff	35
paraphernalia	3	seminary	20	wondrous	15
paraprofessional	3	serrated	16		
parasite	3	sextet	9		
participate	28	shoddy	5		
penetrate	7	shrivel	28		
perimeter	3	siesta	26		
periodic	3	sight	14		